IGNORE PRICE

Strategies of Winning Edge companies that create profitable deals that last.

Frank Kondrot

First Edition

LAGUNA GROUP®

Laguna Niguel, California

Copyright ©2001 by Frank Kondrot

First Edition

First Printing, December 2001

This publication is designed to provide accurate and authoritative information in regard to the subject matter covered. It is sold with the understanding that the publisher is not engaged in rendering legal, accounting, or other professional services. If legal or other expert assistance is required, the services of a competent professional person should be sought.

From a Declaration of Principles jointly adopted by a Committee of the American Bar Association and a Committee of Publishers.

If you do not wish to be bound by the above, you may return this book to the publisher for a full refund.

Library of Congress Control Number: 2001098351

ISBN: 0-9715308-0-7

Printed in Hong Kong

Ordering Information

This book and other publications are available by ordering from Laguna Group at (949) 240-9069, or **www.lagunagroup.com.**

Discounts on bulk quantities are available.

This book is dedicated to my loving wife, Sue, my partner for life; and our children, Kevin and Kristen, who have made our life's journey stimulating.

Contents

Acknowledgments

I have been blessed during my life and career by guidance and support from family, friends, colleagues and my elite business connections. To list each one would require more space than is available. I sincerely thank them all.

For unique contributions, a special thanks to:

Esther Y. Kim, Attorney at Law - (714) 771-3613 - for her peer review and advice on the legal topics. I worked with her in my corporate days, and hope to continue our professional association.

Brian Burton Design - (949) 786-6333 - who designed the book cover and our Laguna Group materials. He has the patience of a saint.

John Garcia, whose invaluable advice and guidance over the years is not forgotten.

Nathan Roberts, nathanr@tardislabs.com, for his kind permission to reproduce his entropy artwork shown in Figure 8.1. He did not charge a fee, unlike Time, Inc.

Last but not least, my Saturday golf group, the camaraderie and the weekly game with them is priceless.

THE EVOLUTION OF BUSINESS DEALS - WHAT'S SPARKING THE CHANGE?

Rules Have Changed

Information & Technology

Stakeholders

Behavior Shift

Fads come and go, but lasting change takes hold in business culture as a result of steady evolution. Twenty years ago, the concepts in this book might have been viewed as too revolutionary, but today many factors have come together to make them timely and well-tested. Size of the company does not matter. Fortune 50 firms to Fortune "wannabe" organizations now recognize that *negotiating the relationship* is the cornerstone of business.

Companies that recognize this quantum shift in deal making that is now going on will profit by it. The information age, new technology, and a more highly-educated work force have shifted the way things are done in business. It is almost the evolutionary equivalent of the leap from monkey to man.

Consider this recent example of deal making: Lisa, the primate specialist at the Columbus Zoo, observed that one of their gorillas, Colo, was hiding something in her hand. Concerned that she might have gotten something from a visitor that could hurt her, Lisa approached the gorilla with some fruit, hoping to exchange it for the item Colo grasped. Calmly talking and gesturing to the animal, the keeper finally got Colo to show what she was holding—a lady's charm bracelet. Relieved that it was not anything worse, Lisa still wanted to take the charm bracelet away from Colo to make sure she did not swallow it.

The keeper offered Colo the piece of fruit, indicating that she wanted to trade. Colo looked at the charm bracelet, then at the fruit, and back to the charm bracelet as if pondering the trade. Lisa again pointed to the piece of the fruit and then the charm bracelet, this time offering the fruit in one hand while holding her other hand open. Finally Colo took the fruit but, much to Lisa's surprise, Colo broke off just one of the charms and gave it to her. The gorilla then coyly displayed the bracelet to Lisa, pointed to the remaining basket of fruit, and back to the bracelet in her hand. Colo knew she had something Lisa wanted, and had figured out that trading the pieces of the bracelet would get her more fruit.

This primitive concept of negotiating a deal goes far back into prehistoric times. Some business organizations are still doing deals at the simplest levels, like Colo, the gorilla. Each transaction is viewed as a one-shot deal, not realizing how one negotiation might impact the next in a series. Others have discovered the emerging facets of negotiating business "relationships" instead of just transactions and are capitalizing on these new concepts.

What is initiating these changes?

The Rules Have Changed

Large corporations dominated the business landscape twenty years ago. Their size and profit margins often concealed many mistakes. The expression, "flood waters cover a lot of stumps," was an appropriate description of the way business was conducted. Today the fat has been cast off, margins are thinner, and the companies dominating world markets are strikingly different. This has led to an increased focus on the bottom line, and pressure on employees to hit performance targets. Some employees interpreted the make-a-profit message as "make a profit at any cost."

The profit-at-all cost approach to deal making by some employees has left some companies in unfortunate situations. Wal-Mart conducted an independent study and found that some of their major suppliers were giving lower prices to their competitors. This news shocked Wal-Mart since their marketing strategy is to build a reputation as the low-price leader. The supplier sales personnel were reacting to the combative and demeaning tactics the Wal-Mart buyers had used over the years — getting price concessions without regard to the human element.

The message was very clear, the suppliers felt better about dealing with organizations that treated them with respect and trust. They were happy to give those other organizations their best deals.

Focusing on your profit, or on one-dimensional negotiations that deal with price alone, cause each side to defend their own profit. As times get tough, and companies worry about survival, the natural tendency is to go after their suppliers' profits first.

One of the first companies I worked for had a division that produced tissues-culture media, an important tool for medical research. The biggest selling product in that category was the Rhesus Monkey Kidney cell line.

To learn about our manufacturing procedures, I visited the company facility and the animal handlers who worked with the Rhesus monkeys. They had to extract the monkey's kidney to produce the cell culture. The handler had to go into the caged area to bring out a monkey to sacrifice for the procedure.

You can imagine how this looked to the uninitiated observer. These monkeys are naturally vicious, with sharp teeth that can inflict serious damage. So the handler would suit up in protective padded clothing, heavy gloves, and a wire mesh helmet for protection before entering the monkey cage. The handler indicated to me that something unique always happened when he went in the cage and asked me to watch closely. As he entered the cage I observed a large Rhesus monkey cautiously approach the handler. The handler slowly walked toward the large monkey and extended his arms. The large monkey darted to one side, snatched a smaller monkey, and thrust it into the handler's arms. The handler then left the cage with the squirming smaller monkey, amid a cacophony of monkey screeches and howls from all over the cage. It was pretty simple, the large monkey had it all figured out: Monkeys leave the cage and never return - so take this small guy instead of me!

This is a great example of the animal kingdom's survival instinct. This trait must be imbedded in our genetic structure. Without this survival instinct, our species would have disappeared a long time ago. This powerful natural force is at work in today's businessperson. Even modern theories like EQ (Emotional Intelligence) have a hard time overcoming our instinct for self-preservation.

Give and Take in the negotiation will shift into more of the *Take* and less of the *Give* as people gravitate toward pushing hard in the deal to get more for their own side. The phrase "Win-Win" becomes more of a tactic than a relationship-building approach. The old business paradigm was to use negotiation like a weapon, bluff if you do not have legitimate reasons, withhold information and deceive your opponent, yet obtain the others' confidential information even if by questionable methods. Squeeze the other side to boost your bottom line.

Ignatio Lopez, VP of purchasing at General Motors from 1992 - 1993, conducted some of the most egregious examples of squeezing the supplier. Lopez had some great business ideas, including his model manufacturing Plant X, a super-efficient factory, but sadly he will remain infamous for what most call his unethical business practices. During his brief reign, he went to long-standing GM suppliers and even subsidiaries demanding that they submit additional bids on existing business, and then to re-bid again, and then re-bid again and again — in an attempt to cut his costs.

He then went to GM's Strategic Alliance Partners and threatened to take the parts and designs that they had jointly and confidentially worked on for years and put them out to competitive bid unless they lowered their prices by five percent across the board.

The contracts the Partners had with GM were considered exclusive and they openly shared proprietary information to enable each side to work on quality improvement and cost reduction. Often teams of cost-cutting and engineering experts from GM were invited to view the Partners' manufacturing processes and secrets. In short, Lopez went about brazenly ignoring the existing rules on pricing, on contract terms, on internal/external suppliers, and the rules on intellectual property. Lopez openly went on to patent this purchasing process of gaining access to confidential information and then squeezing the supplier.

The parts manufacturers were so offended by this breach of trust that some of the relationships have not been repaired to this day. Suppliers nicknamed him "Lopez the Terrible" and the "Russelsheim Strangler" for these tactics. It is interesting to note that as of this writing, Mr. Lopez is facing civil and criminal litigation with General Motors and AG Volkswagen for allegedly stealing confidential GM documents. Perhaps he never read the bible quote, "for whatever a man sows, this he will also reap."

These old rules did appear to garner a profit for one side. The question now asked by many business executives is "But at what cost?"

Information and Technology

Business-to-business dealing is evolving at an increasing pace. New tools enable us to do things in a fraction of the time it took years ago. Cell phones, PDAs, faster computers, and Internet access are dramatically changing the way business information is transferred.

In 1965, Gordon Moore, co-founder of Intel, observed that the number of transistors per square inch on computer boards had doubled every year since the integrated circuit was invented. This trend will continue, Moore predicted. Data density has doubled approximately every 18 months since 1965, enabling computers to process at ever-faster speeds. This is known as Moore's Law, and to put it into perspective the chart below (Figure 1.1) illustrates the doubling effect from 64 transistors on a microchip starting in 1965. (I couldn't fit the bar for the year 2001 on this page as it would be 5,485 feet higher than the 1977 bar!)

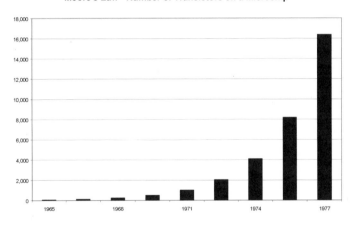

Moore's Law - Number of Transistors on a Microchip

Figure 1.1

Industry experts expect Moore's Law to hold for at least another two decades. Think of the acceleration of information processing and the resulting impact on business deal-making these technological advancements will have.

Let us look at the impact increased access to information and technology has had on even the simplest of business transactions, the commodity negotiation. In terms of total international trade, coffee is now the second most valuable commodity on earth, surpassed only by oil.

Eighty years ago, when coffee brokers dealt with the growers by visiting them high in the Columbian mountains, the negotiations were very one-sided. The coffee broker knew the spot market price for coffee — vital information the grower did not have ready access to. He could only rely on age-old negotiating tactics to try and raise the buyer's paltry offer. When the deal was made, the grower would always wonder, "How much money did I leave on the table?"

With the advent of radio, the grower gained contact with the outside world and, more importantly, access to current commodity prices for coffee on the international exchanges.

The Kefa region of southern Ethiopia, where coffee first grew and derived its name, is one of the most remote areas of the world. Yet even there, the government-controlled radio broadcasts daily market prices. This helps to level the field with the brokers who buy the top-quality beans sold in trendy coffee shops like Starbucks across the developed world.

The coffee market has fluctuated wildly in the last few years, yet certain growers get double or triple the commodity price for their coffee, even in the low markets. Today with Internet access and wireless technology, the balance of power has shifted. Information is flowing faster and is becoming harder to withhold as a bargaining lever.

Today people enter the work force with more formal education than previous generations. Looking at the current statistics, the number of high school students going on to college in the US in 1965 was 51% or nearly six-million students. By 2001, the numbers had jumped to 65% or 15-million going to college.

Sixty years ago, an applicant for a management position who had a college degree or beyond was a rarity; today, it is considered the entry level of education in most corporations.

Business dealmakers today are considered to be more knowledgeable. More importantly, they know how and where to look for information. The ability to quickly access information from a variety of sources is one of the big drivers in changing the business deal-making environment.

Stakeholders

The number of stakeholders influencing organizational strategy is growing. Consider the environmental and animal-rights activists, and their increasing influence on companies today.

A case in point: McDonald's. The gigantic burger chain decided to become a world leader in social responsibility. This decision led them to yield to pressure from People for the Ethical Treatment of Animals (PETA) to only buy eggs from ranchers who treat their chickens humanely.

McDonald's recently sent letters to all its egg suppliers demanding that they comply with strict new rules: Each egg-laying hen must now have 72-square-inches of space (an increase of about 50% over the industry standard), suppliers must stop the practice of withdrawing food or water to stimulate molting (which increases egg production), and stop beak trimming. They were given until the end of 2001 to comply or risk losing sales of roughly two billion eggs.

The egg producers felt betrayed by this shift in requirements because they had responded to earlier pressures from McDonald's and other major buyers to produce eggs at lower cost. In the current market, most suppliers are just breaking even, and now are looking at adding between 15 and 20 cents per dozen to their production costs to comply with the new guidelines. They are perplexed to say the least.

Any producer knows that unhappy and unhealthy hens do not lay eggs. As demanded by customers who want to buy eggs at ever-lower prices, the producers selected the best and most efficient methods available. Some of them resent this outside interference and are kicking up a storm of protest, hoping to get McDonald's to change its mind.

The more savvy egg ranchers saw this change coming. They knew that PETA had campaigns focusing on Burger King, Wendy's, KFC, and even the supermarket chains including Albertsons, Kroger, and Safeway.

The savvy egg ranchers had been watching the developing trends and were intent on keeping ahead of the change curve. They knew that complying with the new guidelines would give them a bargaining advantage. As in most other industries, they are finding that in today's changing business environment, low cost is not the only factor in sales success.

Another example is Taco Bell, famous for their delicious, but somewhat fattening Mexican-style fast food. Under pressure from health organizations, they launched a low-fat line of burritos and tacos. The product was good, but sales were dismal. One of the main reasons is that Taco Bell's core customers are young adults who are not worried about calorie intake. Quite simply, they did not want that kind of product.

The cost to Taco Bell for this failed program was in the millions — for developing the product, marketing it, and training their franchise stores. Some experts say the company should have stonewalled the health groups, and refused to let outsiders dictate company strategy.

I recommend another solution: Engage well-meaning outsiders in a dialogue. Let them see Taco Bell's viewpoint, and then negotiate a more cost-effective approach.

Many lessons were learned by these attempts to please outside pressure groups, but the lasting impact on corporate strategy is clear. Decades ago, organizations functioned with a rubber-stamp board and silent shareholders, seemingly unencumbered by outside interference. The old linear model of Supplier - Organization - Customer may become extinct.

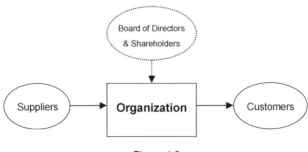

Figure 1.2

Today, organizations have active boards, vocal shareholder and investor groups, and numerous emergent stakeholder factions. These stakeholder groups have learned to exert leverage at multiple points of the Supplier-Organization-Customer chain. Styrofoam containers have all but vanished from fast food stores due to organized pressure from the environmental groups. Even a dominant company like Microsoft learned they were not immune to stakeholder groups' organized campaigns. Their recent antitrust lawsuits snowballed because of orchestrated lobbying by competitor stakeholders. Many new points of influence now shape organization decision-making. Figure 1.3 illustrates how the new model is much more complex.

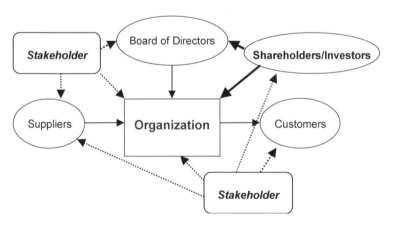

Figure 1.3

In addition to the customers, suppliers, and shareholders - now the external *stakeholders* are a growing segment who need to be negotiated with and managed.

Behavior Shift

Good behavior is making a positive comeback in business. Some experts say it's the passing of the World War II management style - expecting obedience and respect without question. Some say that members of the more enlightened and educated workforce are willing to trust their own judgment first instead of blindly following someone else's direction. The trend is toward a more businesslike and reasoning approach to deal making. Threats and tantrums, the weapons of the bully, are not tolerated any more.

A great example of this was the experience of a manager at a Jersey City, NJ Ryder Truck rental location. One of their busy seasons is the week of Valentine's Day, when local florists and balloon bouquet vendors need rental delivery vans to keep up with the heavy seasonal demand.

One particularly rude customer stuck out in the manager's memory. Not only was this man abusive to the employees at the rental store the first day he rented a van, but he returned the next day to complain about a broken mirror. He demanded immediate repair and insisted he be served ahead of other customers. In addition to screaming at the clerk, he went out of his way to be rude to everyone in the store. He came back two days later, very angry, reported that his van was stolen and wanted his cash deposit refunded - right then. He also claimed that since the truck was stolen the day before, he wasn't going to pay for the extra day it took him to come back to the store.

Store policy required a police report on the stolen van to issue a refund, so after much protesting he left to file the police report. Returning three days later with the police report, he escalated the negotiation. He had put $25 worth of gas in the van before it was stolen, and now wanted the rental agency to refund that money also. He moaned and complained about the inconvenience, and how it was the agency's fault. After much protesting, he finally agreed to split the difference on the tank of gas.

The story takes an interesting twist here. This was 1993, and the FBI investigation into the first World Trade Tower bombing in New York City had uncovered pieces of a truck used to transport the explosives. It was a yellow Ford Econoline Van, and the vehicle identification number on a fragment of the frame matched the van reported stolen from the New Jersey Ryder Truck rental agency, which had been rented to the rude customer. The Ryder executives who gave Mohammad Salameh his $400 cash deposit refund were actually FBI agents. He was promptly arrested and the contract was found to have traces of nitrate on it, linking it to a person who had contact with explosives. The Ryder Truck manager stated that the rude and obnoxious behavior of Salameh made him stand out and ultimately led to his swift arrest.

Who hasn't had to deal with an abusive egomaniac in a business deal? A common feeling after such a negative experience is the decision to never deal with them again. In fact, most people hope that person gets his comeuppance, and want to watch it happen.

Revenge is a powerful emotion, and its negative energy should not have a place in business today. Some even argue that these short-term emotional bully tactics are not effective with the more educated businesspeople.

They can see right through those characters.

Most major companies are now instituting programs to retrain their contracts teams to a more civil and effective style of business negotiating.

THE SHIFT TOWARD SIGNIFICANCE AND WORTH

Classic Price Perspective

Purchasing and Management Trends

Customer Perspective

Worth in the Distribution Chain

A major trend in business over the last decade is that large companies are reducing the number of their suppliers. Digital Equipment carved out 67% of their suppliers, Motorola dropped 70%, and Xerox reduced the supplier roles by 90%! These firms have found that working closely with a smaller group of suppliers increases quality and is more efficient over time.

Suppliers are also evaluating customers with an eye on the bottom line. Unprofitable and difficult customers who become a drain on a suppliers profits and resources are now culled out. In our seminars we recommend putting the bottom 20% on probation; either they turn around or you turn them over to your competition. Just "good" is no longer enough to survive; today the expectation is exceptional performance at all levels. Now begins the difficult task — how do you keep the valuable business relationship?

All business relationships have a common element — products or services are exchanged for currency of one kind or another. Research indicates that perceptions of this "exchange" vary between the participants. Long-held truisms that defined negotiating narrowly along buyer and seller roles are now under scrutiny. Let us look at some of the shifts and their sources.

Classic Price Perspective

The equation that helps us understand this business transaction from the supplier's perspective:

$$\text{Cost} + \text{Profit} = \textbf{Price}$$

Cost
Cost is the sum of the investments the supplier expends in the development of the product. Depending on the type of business it might include things such as raw materials, labor, facilities, overhead, R&D, marketing, customer and/or technical support, distribution, and sales costs.

Profit
Profit, the supplier's reward, is both the incentive and the means to produce more of the product. Some organizations have a target profit amount (gross profit percentage, flat rate, fixed dollar amount, and so on). Sadly, there are some

companies that just count what is left over after the negotiation. Making a profit is vital for survival. The United States tax code states that to be considered a valid business it must make profit in 3 out of 5 years — or it is considered a hobby!

Price

Price is the visible unit negotiated in business deals. It is the scorecard for both sides. ***Often neither side really knows the true profit and cost, so the focus is on price.*** The supplier views a reduced price as a cut in his profit, the variable impacted directly if he reduces the price. The customer wants a lower price so his transactional profit will increase. This price focus is regarded by most as the one-dimensional mode that all transactional deals encompass.

In this classic price perspective, the customers attempt to negotiate a lower price is often viewed by the supplier as an attack on profits.

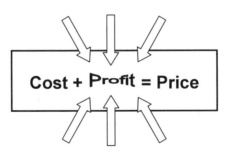

Assuming the supplier is running a lean organization, a lower price results in a smaller profit.

Some companies keep lowering prices to meet customer demands until they cannot survive. Such a course also has pitfalls for the customer, who will put their suppliers out of business if they take away the supplier's profit-making ability.

An example of this was an ambulance and patient transport company that won an exclusive contract with a large regional managed care organization (MCO). The ambulance company submitted a very low bid with the hope of getting their foot in the door and then raising rates in subsequent years. During the contract renewal negotiations, they got beat up pretty badly. Not wanting to walk away from the business after only one year, the owner caved-in on pricing demands and signed up for another year.

Besides demanding additional services and routes that stretched the ambulance company's resources beyond reason, the MCO played the accounts-payable game. They routinely held up invoice payments beyond 120 days, challenging each item and demanding additional backup for every invoice. Nine months into the contract's second year, the difficult situation the MCO was forcing on the ambulance company became impossible.

"We'll be out of business in three days," the ambulance company's owner informed the MCO's president. "The banks are impounding all our vehicles and equipment. I hate to admit failure, but I have no other option. We're declaring bankruptcy."

Caught by surprise—the ambulance company's warnings and complaints had been ignored—the managed care organization scrambled to contract with other ambulance firms in the area. However, word was out on the street about the bankruptcy and the MCO's payment tactics — and no one wanted their business. The managed care company had to loan (actually donate) money to the ambulance company to keep them afloat for another six months. It cost the managed care company far more to bail out the ambulance company than they had temporarily saved with the new contract.

In business deals, focusing on the narrow objective of cost reduction through price negotiation may obstruct an organization's view of the bigger picture.

Suppliers can get caught in an embarrassing situation when loyal customers discover that the price they are currently paying is higher than what is offered to new customers. An example of this was the cellular phone packages offered over the last few years. Once you signed up with a company and locked into a one or two year contract, you would soon see rates offered to new customers lower than your deal. And as if to add "insult to injury", they even threw in a free phone to that new customer!

The mail order clothing companies also came under fire for sending catalogues with different prices based on zip code or whether you were an existing customer or not. This was an attempt to attract new customers with some loss-leader-pricing, but it angered existing customers who did not share in the same opportunity.

Airlines are blatant culprits with their advertising campaigns promoting lower prices to the leisure traveler who can stay over a Saturday night, while the loyal business travelers pay the top prices - unwillingly funding the leisure travelers' discounts.

This application of price to attract customers can create problems because of the perceived unfairness to loyal customers - the suppliers' supposed friends. This is called the cliff effect in pricing. Existing loyal customers pay gradually higher prices over time, or steady prices, as the market prices drop. A gap soon develops between existing customer pricing and promotions to attract new customers. This disparity is comparable to a steadily rising hill that comes to an abrupt drop off - the cliff - and when existing customers hit the edge - see the gap in pricing - they usually go away fuming.

Focusing on price in such a narrow way can cause suppliers to lose sight of the profits in their existing base of business customers.

Price and Satisfaction

Over the last ten years I have conducted a study of negotiation behaviors by thousands of business executives who have attended my seminars. At the conclusion of one of the exercises, the participants rate their satisfaction with the settlement price of the deal and it is then compared to the relative profit. A supplier receiving a higher price rates this as high profit for him/ herself, while a customer getting a lower price would also rate this as high profit for him/herself - it is all relative to your position in the exercise. The chart in Figure 2.1 shows the typical plotted pattern of the responses.

From the data it appears that there is no correlation between price and satisfaction ratings.

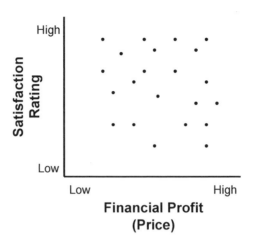

Figure 2.1

Ask yourself these questions about your business:

♦ Do you have a customer who is getting the deal-of-the-century - the best pricing available - yet they are still unhappy?

♦ Do you have a customer who is paying full list price, no discounts of any kind and is happy-as-a-clam?

People getting a great deal should be well satisfied, and those paying the most should be less happy, right? So in each of the above questions you would expect a "no" response concerning their satisfaction with the deal. Did you answer yes to both questions? How could some customers have such a contrary reaction; since we are led to believe price is such an important aspect in the buying process?

In the real business world, through countless interviews with business executives, and critical reviews of both failed and successful deals - all indicators appear to confirm that price does not necessarily drive satisfaction in a business deal.

"He is well paid who is well satisfied" -William Shakespeare

Price is an independent and apparently unrelated factor; to increase satisfaction, focus more on the "process" of the deal-making.

Purchasing and Management Trends

Business organizations are continuing to evolve, searching for ways to reduce costs and offer more value to their end customer. This places stress on current thinking and practices of traditional purchasing. A joint research initiative was started in 1998 by the Center for Advanced Purchasing Studies and the National Association of Purchasing Management to identify these trends as they attempt to align themselves with the new organizational objectives. Some of the emerging paradigm shifts within purchasing functions are:

Strategic Sourcing
The goal is to maximize leverage and flexibility throughout the supply chain by select alliances. Organizations are taking different approaches. Gallo, one of the largest wine companies, does not grow grapes anymore. Nike does not manufacture a single running shoe, choosing instead to outsource its entire shoe production overseas. They are a growing segment that lives by the credo, "If we are not the best in the world

at an activity, if it is not our core competency, and if it does not allow us to differentiate ourselves to our customers, then we should outsource it to someone who is best in the world." Reebok, by contrast, still builds shoes in its Massachusetts facilities, finding that manufacture in the US gives them a strategic advantage on design and time-to-market. Large and small companies alike are scrutinizing the supply chain, looking for advantages.

The Outsourcing of Non-Strategic Internal Functions

Accounting, law, human resources, office supplies and equipment, and maintenance are some of the traditional functions now under close scrutiny for outsourcing. Companies are looking at each point in the value chain; if they are not the best at it, they find a supplier who is. Some consider Royal Dutch Shell as the world's best managed oil company; they outsource their long-range strategic planning.

Combined Supplier/Customer Relationship Management

Some organizations are considering pooling a cross-functional management team in one office to leverage and focus more on the relationship management process and knowledge. Transaction tracking will be de-emphasized. With increased effort expended in the human-to-human element for both suppliers and customers, the new approach will rely more on automated systems to achieve enhanced results.

Supply-Chain Partner Selection and Contribution

Everyone is looking for cost improvement opportunities to expand their business and become more efficient through cooperation and process improvements. If a partner is not making a significant contribution to your business success, they are ripe for replacement.

The organization model is shifting from the old linear supplier-customer model to the emerging dynamic organization model shown below.

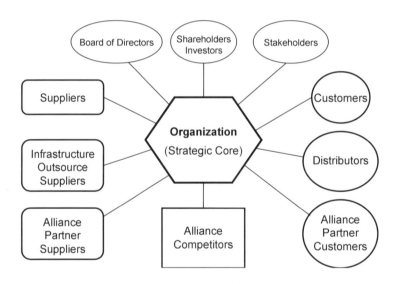

Figure 2.2

Alliances with suppliers, customers and competitors will become commonplace. Combined with new channels of distribution, the traditional lines defining buyer and seller will blur. There are many opinions on the timing of these changes and possible organizational structures. The above diagram shows just one of the many options on the horizon.

One element is consistently found in all the potential models: the suppliers of the future will be fewer in number, and being of world-class caliber will be a requirement. To achieve greater efficiency and quality, organizations are paring the ranks of their suppliers. If we look at the spectrum of a company supplier list, it shows a typical bell curve distribution:

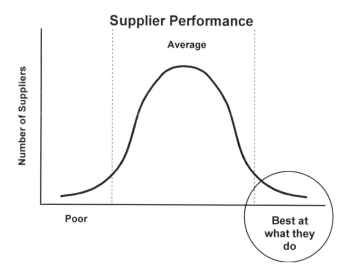

Figure 2.3

The challenge for a supplier is to move into the top performance level. They must be *significant* performers and contributors to be considered world-class. Significance is defined by the importance and uniqueness of what they offer in the deal. Are suppliers contributing to their customer's success? Is there a real impact on the other side's business effectiveness?

The suppliers in the lower performance categories will not survive the imminent cut. One of the most chilling observations is that supplier organizations who are "best at what they do" today, may lose their hold on excellence unless they keep step with the evolving business models.

The purchasing mentality impacts an organization's effectiveness right at the start of the supply chain. Does your organization tend to get the lowest prices and then pick the best vendor from the lowest responders — "the best of the bunch from the bottom of the barrel?" Or is your strategy to find the best suppliers in a field and then use the bidding process to benchmark prices?

These fundamental shifts in business practices and deal making are impacting both supplier and customer organizations.

Customer Perspective

Consideration of customer perspective leads us to profound questions:

How do business customers really view the transaction equation?

What does the customer really want from a supplier in a business deal? Is it just a low price?

Although the answer most frequently given by business procurement professionals over the years has been *low price,* new evidence shows that many of those answers may have been a negotiation smoke screen. In markets where low prices were offered as the only differentiator, research showed that those companies failed miserably to gain significant market share. The conclusion in study after study is clear: business customers are reluctant to buy on low price alone.

With the growth of the Internet and the B2B (business to business) segment, surveys conducted repeated these earlier findings showing that nearly 80% of corporate purchasing departments would not buy on low price alone. They placed a strong brand or reliable customer service ahead of low price as a preference for doing business. It appears that price is only decisive if all other things are equal.

The common theme in guiding companies today as to what products they buy — or what suppliers they want to be associated with — is the concept of value. Value is sometimes hard to define, unless we look at the buying equation a new way.

$$\text{Price} + \textbf{Worth} = \text{Value}$$

Price
The deal tariff, the currency exchanged for product, is same as in the earlier equation.

Worth
These are the tangible and intangible things that define the reasons for choosing one buying option over another. This defines what the product can do directly for the customer; it is the benefits, the unique solution, and the holistic sum of the product attributes. This is what the customer views as the real *significance* of your business transaction. To be viewed as a world-class

supplier, you must offer significant *worth* to the customer.

Value

This is the hard-to-describe intangible that sums up the customer's perceived benefits from the deal. Most find it hard to concretely define the concept of value. Some experts claim that to describe *value* you need to move more into the emotional side of the process. Many define value as "The *feeling* a person is willing to exchange money for." In business, value perceptions are formed by the combination of both logical and emotional worth components.

The important component to focus on is *worth*, the element driving the value of the business.

Worth in the Distribution Chain

The Tupperware Corporation is a $1.1 billion multinational organization producing premium food storage, preparation, and serving items in more than 100 countries. The founder, Earl Tupper, a DuPont chemist, started working with a new polyethylene plastic in 1942. He produced a line of home plastic food storage containers, and his marketing edge was simulating the inversed rim of a paint can to get an airtight seal. Most of us are familiar with the "Tupperware burp" of escaping air as the lid is sealed on the container.

Tupper originally sold his products to consumers from retail store shelves with mixed success. One of the problems was the classic distribution chain; it presented nightmares to his and other companies of the time. Each step in the chain added to the cost, but may or may not have contributed to the customer's perception of worth. In fact, some steps in the distribution chain decreased the perceived worth through poor customer service, lack of inventory, wrong markets, or high price markups. The chart shows potential impact on worth perception:

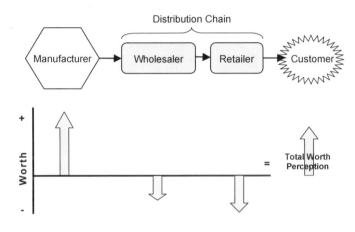

Figure 2.4

The challenge to Tupper was to find a way to keep the worth high through the distribution chain. His breakthrough came when he experimented with hiring women to sell the product directly. At the time, large numbers of women were entering the workforce, but most were not finding much in the way of meaningful jobs. The direct selling approach was a quick success. When Brownie Wise joined Tupperware, she was a single mother with a flare for marketing and great people skills. She became a sensation in 1951 by introducing the world to a new idea: direct selling Tupperware at neighborhood parties. This direct-selling system launched Tupperware into the record books. Tupperware parties swiftly moved into legend; today one of them starts every two seconds somewhere in the world. Its most important contribution to distribution strategy is that this system actually adds significant worth-perception to the end customer.

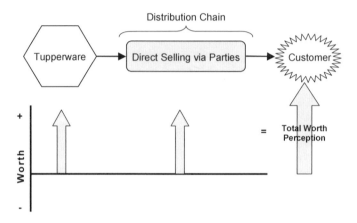

Figure 2.5

The complex distribution systems emerging today make it important to challenge each link in the chain from suppliers through distribution. As JIT (Just-in-Time) manufacturing or supplier alliances move into the chain, each new link adds to or subtracts from the total worth. Some large corporations are forming purchasing consortiums for bargaining leverage and efficiencies, which can be a plus, but on the downside they can restrict access to new suppliers and ideas. Some parts of the chain compete with each other, which can be good and bad. Tupperware recently decided to form a distribution alliance with Target Stores, selling its products in a retail environment in addition to its independent distributors. One thing is certain, change will continue.

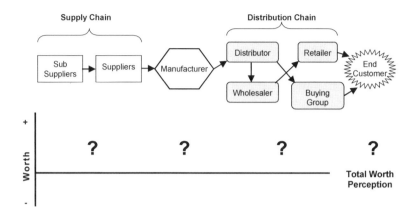

Figure 2.6

Each link impacts the total chain and the end customer only perceives the sum total of the worth. If your organization uses a channel or distributors to reach the end customer, consider these questions for your organization:

- Is each link adding worth or just extracting a "toll" along the chain?

- Is each link adding or subtracting to the end customer's worth perception?

- Are there any redundant links?

- Is the end customer clear on how to find your product, or are the links confusing them?

The shift in generating *worth awareness* has an exponentially greater impact on the customer's perception of value than does reducing price.

WHAT'S REALLY BEING NEGOTIATED?

Trust

Trust Life Cycle

Fatal Investment Thinking

The focus is now on the end game—what is the optimum result you can obtain in a particular business relationship? This forward thinking by the business greats highlight the importance of thinking through the competitive parts of business dealing and asking the vital question, "What am I *really* negotiating in this deal?" The hidden price that people and companies pay when they focus on just the short term is devastating.

Trust

Bob flew into his company's Miami headquarters to interview for the Marketing Manager job—this would be a big promotion for him. He planned for the day of interviews, brought copies of all his glowing performance reviews, rehearsed his accomplishments, and planned answers for those trick questions such as, "Tell me about your weaknesses," or "What thing in your career are you most unhappy about?" After the grueling day of interviews with all the key executives and dinner with the company president, Bob was proud of the way he had presented himself, not missing a question or an opportunity to show his good side. He felt he had the job locked.

The Vice President of Marketing invited him to join him and the other marketing mangers for a round of golf the next day, before he took his flight home. Bob enthusiastically agreed. He loved golf, and felt it would be an opportunity to score more points, showing them that he was a real competitor, a can-do-guy who would be perfect for the job. Bob played well, won the side bets, told great jokes, and was very friendly to all. On the flight home he was sure he cinched the promotion and would be in an excellent position to negotiate a good salary and relocation package when the job was offered to him.

After the round of golf while Bob was flying home, the VP of Marketing had a brief meeting with his team to discuss Bob. While they found him to have exceptional skills, motivation, and so on, they were all troubled by some minor observations on the golf course. Each of them had observed times when Bob reported a lower score on a hole than they thought he actually made. They were in disblief when he claimed to find his ball on the other side of a lake — a 300-plus yard carry that even Tiger Woods would have had problems with, or the time when Bob disappeared into the bushes to find his ball they were surprised, that after hearing three or four whacks, the ball flew magically onto the fairway without the sound of a hit.

It was only a friendly game with one-dollar bets, but they all had doubts concerning Bob's integrity. The VP decided not to extend the job offer to Bob, stating that if he could not trust him in a little game of golf, what would he be like when the pressure was really on?

This is a classic example of a person not understanding the *big picture* in business. A lot has been published on how to *position* yourself, or how to gain *power* while negotiating. Usually the number one nagging question people ask themselves after any negotiation is, *"Did I leave any money on the table?"* Understandably, our competitive nature and some lack of confidence gives rise to this approach and that follow-up question.

The real focus should be on the follow-up question, which often is quickly passed over because it makes us uncomfortable: *"How well did I really do?"*

To answer the second question with a reasonable degree of validity, you must get to the core issue of repeat business: people want to deal with people they can trust.

Like it or not, we are being judged every day in business. Most of us do not like to be categorized. The famous British actor Ewan McGregor, of *Star Wars* and *Trainspotting,* had this comment on the Hollywood system: "The system makes me sick sometimes. They put actors onto A, B, and C lists, according to how much money each person can make for the studio, and I just think: 'How dare you do that? We're not a bunch of letters to make you money — we're people.'" While I empathize with Mr. McGregor to a point, that same rating system has made him a personal fortune, as I am sure he knows.

The Hollywood rating system is in the nature of how we grade any person in any profession. We do not necessarily place people on dollar-defined lists; instead, we have many sets of mental classifications that we assign to people in their various capacities. It happens automatically, usually very quickly, and often it is based on very little reliable evidence because we may not have access to any other kind.

In business, the issue of trust is similar but a whole lot simpler — there are only two lists you can fall into: people who trust you and those who do not. Getting knocked off the A list onto the B list in business can be fatal for your higher career aspirations.

We are discussing the ongoing test of the business relationship that is always active. Each day your actions are observed and impressions are made. Unfortunately, many people conduct their business as if they do not even know this continuous test is going on.

Trust Life Cycle

There are four distinct phases of a business life cycle, which is to say, of the trust involved:

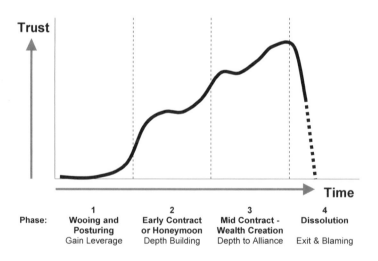

| Phase: | 1 Wooing and Posturing Gain Leverage | 2 Early Contract or Honeymoon Depth Building | 3 Mid Contract - Wealth Creation Depth to Alliance | 4 Dissolution Exit & Blaming |

Figure 3.1

There is only one road into and out of a business relationship, and that road's name is **trust**.

Phase 1: Wooing or Posturing

This is the phase in which you seek to gain leverage. It is the most aggressive phase of nearly all business relationships, fueled by each side's reluctance to fully commit or trust the other side. Most of the time is spent in parading your strengths, trying to get the other side to give-in first. If you are a buyer, you show low interest, pretend there is a lot of competition, and keep stating that only price matters. If you are a seller, you indicate that the product is in short supply because of high demand; you say the price and/or the deal is best now, and may go up later. You put on all the pressure you can to get the buyer to act quickly.

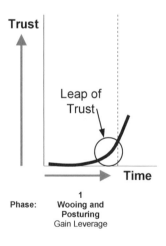

Figure 3.2

Trust is low or non-existent at the early stages of a new business relationship. If the business relationship is to continue (that is, move to phase 2) the seller must assist the buyer to make the critical *leap of trust.* The buyer must have enough faith in the seller's proposed transaction to overcome all past concerns or perceived risks.

At this time, the focus is on a transaction that exchanges money for a product, so it is one-dimensional. Each side is trying to culminate the deal, and maximize their profit at the same time. This makes developing a true win-win deal at this stage improbable because trust between the players is so low.

Some experts say you should minimize the competitive nature in this phase by negotiating a win-win deal. The literature is full of phrases to describe this mind-set: the original *Win-Win,* was a seminal insight when first introduced. *Both Win,* and *Win²* are the identical concept by authors who confuse different sounding with original thinking. *WIN/$_{win}$* seems to imply that my win is more important than your win. I do not want to trivialize the importance of the attempt to keep the competitive stage to a minimum, but let's face it—it is a phase we must go through to get to the next step in the relationship.

It is natural for trust to be low at this point; each side wants to hold power and information close; neither side is willing to share openly because doing so could weaken their position. The best that should be expected in this phase is that each side will discover what is really important to the other side. The aim here should be to cut through the posturing and games, find the real core issues, and make sure that both sides understand them.

Use a negotiating process that encourages each side to want to do business with the other again. They have to trust you to want to continue the relationship.

In a deal that is fair by industry and cultural standards, satisfaction is not driven by the price. It is directly linked to the *way* the negotiation was conducted.

For more on strategy in phase 1, refer to my book, *The Toughest Negotiation.*

Phase 2: Honeymoon, the Early Contract Period

In this phase you pursue Depth Building.

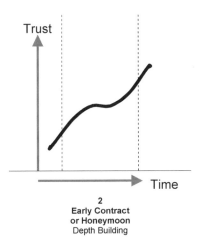

Figure 3.3

During this phase, both sides are pleased that a deal is in effect. Each had to agree, and therefore their egos tell them they made excellent decisions. This is the best time to grow the relationship because each side is visualizing only the favorable aspects of the relationship. To stop working on the relationship at this stage is like giving a plant fertilizer but forgetting to water it. The tactics used in Phase One will determine how successful you can be at this stage. At this phase, many negotiators take the short view and hurt their long-term prospects.

The construction industry is rampant with examples of organizations taking the short-term view after winning a contract. A common practice is to "bid low now, and negotiate your profits later." Under this concept, bidders purposely underbid to win the award, particularly with government agencies that adhere to the outdated low bid mentality. Then the plan is to find mistakes, changes in specs, anything they can use to claim that something was not clear in the original bid, and they need a lot more money to make the changes now.

"I consider change orders to be profits in escrow," one subcontractor told me — and he was not joking. Reputable general contractors might use such people once by mistake, but they never call them again. My favorite expression is, "Pigs get fat, but hogs get slaughtered."

A positive example of building depth early in a relationship concerns Amazon.com as they expanded their offering from books into a myriad of new products. One particularly troublesome area was lawn furniture. This was not the compact, lightweight and easily shipped item like books and CDs. In fact over the Christmas holiday season Jeff Bezos, the founder, was working in one of their distribution stores helping pack boxes to meet the seasonal spike in business. Seeing how long it took them to box each of the lawn furniture pieces, Jeff quickly figured that the labor time in packing ate up all the profit they could make on that item.

Luckily the supplier was keeping close tabs during the early days of the contract with Amazon. After learning of this problem, they suggested that they could box the items separately at their plant before delivery to Amazon's distribution centers, saving time and money for Amazon. The deal was quickly renegotiated, Amazon paying slightly more for the boxing service, but at a fraction of what it would have cost them to box the lawn furniture. And the lawn furniture company covered their cost but increased their value to Amazon in the process— they created additional worth in the relationship with their customer.

The strategy in this phase is to find areas that can turn the relationship from just a one-dimensional transaction into ways that build depth between the parties.

Manufacturers and suppliers intent on developing a Just-In-Time supply management system find the first hurdle is overcoming a built-in resistance to trusting each other. The decades of withholding information, or of using it as a weapon during the price negotiations, appear to be the main culprit.

Trust is becoming the hidden currency of business.

Phase 3: Mid Contract — Wealth Building

In this phase, your strategy should be to take Depth to Alliance Mode.

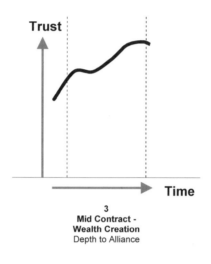

3
**Mid Contract -
Wealth Creation**
Depth to Alliance

Figure 3.4

Focus on worth to keep the deal going. As trust increases, it fosters a climate favoring negotiations to look for ways to create additional wealth for both sides.

Business wealth is defined as the currency of payment — the reward of the deal, and it takes different forms for different people and organizations. Many seek to increase profit, others to gain knowledge, some want to leave a legacy or to foster connections with influential people who can help their careers.

American Hospital Supply Corporation(AHSC), a prime supplier to a major medical center in Alabama, was exploring ways to add value to the relationship. After an extensive review, AHSC discovered that for every dollar spent in buying products (from them or any other supplier) the medical center spent another dollar receiving, storing and moving the product to the patient. AHSC proposed a stockless or JIT (Just-in-Time) venture, whereby they would store all the medical center's supplies in their nearby facility, and deliver to patient bedsides six times a day. Since supply management and logistics was the cornerstone of their business, they were able to do this for only $0.70 vs. the $1.00 currently being spent by the medical center. In addition to the newfound $0.30 profit, the medical center was able to free up much needed space for examination and treatment rooms — making it possible to generate additional revenue.

The deal was a match made in heaven, each party benefited significantly. The medical center cut costs in labor and logistics and, more importantly, added billable revenue from the conversion of the storage space to treatment and research rooms. This was new wealth created for them. As a result of the deal, AHSC gained additional revenue and improved one of their management ratios, RONWA (Return On Net Working Assets). This increased the bonus pool for the division. They also used the medical center as a reference center to display the new service they could now offer their other customers.

The people on the management teams from both sides formed a bond that to this day travels with them. Even as their careers took them to different locations and organizations, they still keep some of the solid career connections made when AHSC worked out their win-win deal with the Alabama medical center.

Phase 4: Dissolution

This Exit and Blaming stage can only be avoided if both sides take responsibility for maintaining trust. Significant drops in trust can be repaired by fast and energetic action that roots out the underlying cause even when doing so costs serious money or involves making painful decisions or difficult admissions. Without such prompt action, the critical moment, the point of no return in the business relationship, becomes a fatal drop of trust.

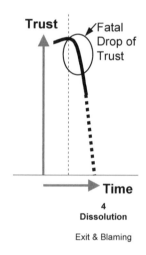

Figure 3.5

Some relationships die quickly — the parts supplier who misses the first shipment, or in any kind of transaction, the quality or service promised does not match what is delivered. Such suppliers move so quickly from phase 1 to 4 that they "don't pass GO, or collect $200." If the situation applies to an individual's performance, they make the B list of negotiators, something that is very hard to overcome for the rest of their career.

Relationships that have stood the test of time are not immune to this harsh reality. Take Ford and Firestone, two partners that started doing business with each other at the beginning of the automotive era. It started as a tight friendship between Harvey Firestone and Henry Ford. The two men would take their families on camping trips together, using the new automobile as the vehicle to transport them to the faraway campsites. The relationship developed into the business venture of Firestone selling tires to Ford for the model-T cars. Firestone became the prime supplier of tires to the Ford Motor Company for the next 100 years, and the family friendship continued right along with the business relationship.

Yet it dissolved abruptly when Firestone experienced a cataclysmic collapse of trust in Ford, specifically about how their customer was handling tire blowout and Ford Explorer issues. It was a messy exit, each side blaming the other for the problem as they both scrambled for PR spin at the other's expense, each hoping to save their own company in the process. In this case, it was the supplier who fired the customer; Firestone announced it was exiting its century-old relationship with Ford, ending one of the oldest automotive business relationships in the world.

Another example is McDonald's, the world's leading food service retailer with about 29,000 restaurants in 121 countries. They recently had to fire the long-time supplier who ran the marketing of their game promotions including *Monopoly* and *Who wants to be a Millionaire?*

The FBI arrested employees of the supplier who allegedly had defrauded McDonald's of more than $13 million over a six-year period. The suspects cornered the winning game pieces and recruited relatives and friends to pose as the winners and collect the prize money.

The statement by McDonald's regarding the termination of the relationship summed it up by saying it was the only responsible course of action considering the magnitude, duration, and lack of meaningful oversight by the supplier. McDonald's, having lost the defrauded $13 million, pledged to give their customers the chance to win every dollar stolen by the criminal ring — a sizeable cost to any company for actions of a once trusted supplier. McDonald's Chairman and CEO, Jack Greenberg, summed up the core issue this way: "We want to emphasize again that McDonald's will do whatever it takes to ensure the integrity of our brand, our restaurants, and the *trust* of our customers."

McDonald's is looking for a new supplier to handle the future promotions, and one thing is certain in the selection process — other factors will carry more weight than the lowest bid.

There is a heightened awareness while exiting the relationship and the potential long-term repercussions. If trust is allowed to fall unchecked, there is a risk of creating an adversary. Figure 3.6 illustrates the drop into extreme distrust, often an unrecoverable situation. Your reputation in the marketplace and the potential for someday regaining that business are linked to preventing this dangerous cascade.

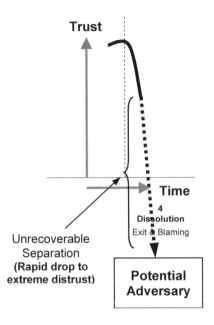

Figure 3.6

In summary, trust in business is fluid. It is not something you gain, and from then on it will see you through any problems that may occur. Just as organizations developed systems to increase manufacturing excellence and quality, they need to implement strategies to ensure the active protection and fostering of trust.

Fatal Investment Thinking

Frontloading the relationship investment ratio can be dangerous to long term survivability. The old way was to "get the product in; they will love us and we will live happily ever after." Somewhat Pollyanna thinking, but it captured the investment philosophy of many marketing programs — a high investment of resources during phase 1 to acquire the relationship; but from then on, little reinvestment to keep it over time.

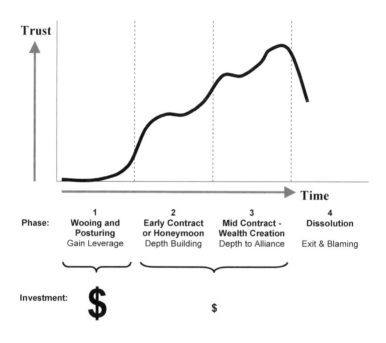

Figure 3.7

Perhaps this sprang from believing in the old adage, "If you build a better mouse trap, the world will beat a path to your door," which implies that a superior product is all you need in business. Whatever validity that concept may have had in the enormously less competitive times of a century ago, it no longer proves out in today's real life.

The better technology does not necessarily become dominant, or even survive. Beta vs. VHS tape format, and Apple vs. DOS operating systems, are two of the best known examples.

Investing in the maintenance of the relationship yields a better return than the money spent to acquire a new customer. The *sunk costs* in the deal will lower the profit during the first two phases; the real earnings will kick in during the later years.

The "Profit of the Deal" increases with time and trust. A graphic portrayal of the relationship value might best be shown in the chart below.

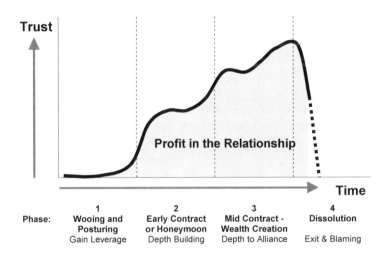

Figure 3.8

Winning Edge business thinking: "Don't merely manage the product, also manage the relationship."

BUSINESS RELATIONSHIP DEPTH

Transactional Mode

Getting Beneath the Surface

Transactional Depth

Friendship Mode

Friendship Depth

The question most organizations face is, "What type of a relationship do I want with each of my customers or suppliers?" There are three potential ways of engaging in a business relationship:

♦ Transactional

♦ Friendship

♦ Alliance

Each mode of business has distinct elements. Given different times and trust levels within each mode there can be unique opportunities to strengthen the relationship, or take it to a higher level.

Transactional Mode

The Transactional Mode underlies all business relationships. Its most primitive form, barter, still exists.

Before the collapse of the USSR, barter was the best way — often the only way — to get things done behind the Iron Curtain. By not buying or selling for rubles, Moscow's corrupt and inefficient Communist bureaucracy could be circumvented. As a result, vast amounts of goods and services were exchanged between the managers of state-owned factories.

In the US today, a tiny fraction of GNP is bartered, either through barter clubs or by direct deals between individuals or companies. The difficulty with barter is that both parties are buyers and sellers, which makes it difficult to precisely match the needs of both as to timing and value.

At an early date, the awkwardness of barter gave rise to currency in the form of coins like those in use today. Although they were unknown in early pharaonic Egypt, coin currency facilitated every sort of transaction well before 300 B.C. (Numismatists — coin collectors — treasure the silver money minted in Alexander the Great's time.) Thus mankind has at least twenty-three hundred years of experience with the Transactional Mode, defined as the buyer exchanging currency for the seller's products or services.

Anywhere in the world you can see this mode in action. The currency might look as different as dollars, drachmas, yen, gold, precious stones, slabs of salt, bronze ingots, or livestock. It will be whatever the local custom defines as the unit of trade.

Most of these principles are as old as history itself, as shown by the earliest decipherable writings yet found by archeologists. On ancient baked clay tablets, bills of sale and other commercial documents are inscribed in Sumerian cuneiform.

The oldest known business still in existence today is the Hoshi Hotel in Japan. Forty-nine generations of the Hoshi family have run their hotel since A.D. 718. Some other notable long-enduring family businesses include:

♦ Barovier & Toso — Venetian glassmakers since 1295

♦ Antinori — Tuscan winemakers since 1385

♦ Beretta — Italian firearm makers since 1526

♦ John Brooke & Sons, Ltd. — English textile weavers since 1541

What do all of these diverse organizations have in common? They have all conducted business successfully for a long time, they have changed with the times, and they continue to earn profits.

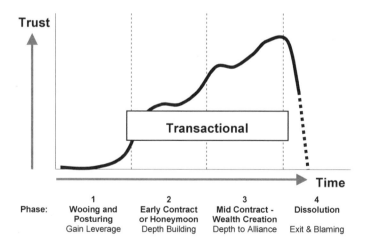

Figure 4.1

This mode is often the best that can be developed with most business-to-business relationships.

The Transactional Mode starts with the Leap of Trust in Phase 1 and can continue through Phase 3. Profit is the measure of either party's success in the Transactional Mode. This mode caries the most risk, on the surface a competitor can always propose a better transactional deal.

Getting Beneath the Surface

With the continuing trend in the reduction of the number of suppliers, and the high cost to acquire new customers - how do you keep existing valuable relationships?

In the second and third phases of the business life cycle, the secret lies in generating worth, which can increase trust and solidify the long-term relationship.

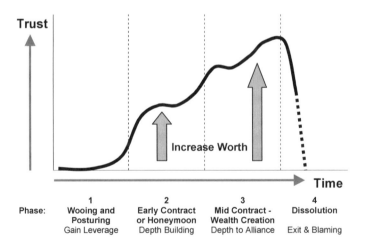

Figure 4.2

The method of keeping a business relationship is to create depth. This means you have to find a way to go beyond just a simple surface transaction that is devoid of emotional impact on either side (X money exchanged for X amount of goods or services) into something notable that can make the relationship stick.

Mission Viejo Motors, an automotive service company I have used for over twenty years, is an example of this. A referral from a friend sent me to them for the first time. Since I trusted my friend's opinion, I was willing to trust Mission Viejo Motors for an initial transaction (Phase 1 relationship). I took my Toyota in for lube, oil change, and general check-up. I had a coupon for a free oil change and filter, and expected to be treated similar to other service stores — they would find something wrong on my car to fix and thereby generate some additional income.

On picking my car up later that day, I was very surprised when one of the owners, Bryan Light, said, "Mr. Kondrot, we changed the oil and filter, checked and filled all fluids, and found everything else okay on the car. No charge today." At first I figured it was a fluke. Could these guys actually be honest?

According to the TV and newspaper articles that always highlight the scam artists, honesty is — or was — a rarity in the automotive repair business. A few days later I received a personal thank-you note from the owners. This was another surprise because—come on, this isn't Nordstrom — it's an automotive repair business! Their pleasant mode of operation repeated the next few transactions — the work was always top quality and always done on time. The personal notes and even a customer satisfaction survey followed. And this was twenty years ago; they were way ahead of their time.

When we planned to get a new car, Mission Viejo Motors offered advice on the models that appeared to be most reliable and had reasonable parts costs, something you do not typically think about in the emotional frenzy of the new car experience. Their advice always turned out to be valuable. All this impressed me, but most importantly, I have kept going back to them for service ever since. They built some depth into our relationship (Phase 2) by enhancing worth. As a result trust increased and that moved the price of their services out of the forefront.

Transactional Depth

Becoming a "Go To"

Many companies consider FedEx as a "Go To" package delivery organization. When it absolutely, positively, has to be there — they use FedEx. There is a famous story of two groups of people in the same Chicago high-rise office building that would ship important documents to each other using FedEx. That meant the package would go from the sending office in Chicago by truck to the airport, be flown to FedEx's Memphis hub, get sorted, be flown back to the Chicago airport, and then go by truck back again to the recipient in Chicago — to the same building, just a different floor. Possibly they did not want to have a receptionist hand deliver sensitive documents, or because their perceived need for a third party paper trail outweighed the extra costs. Bottom line, those folks had more confidence in FedEx than in the building's own mail courier system!

Increase the worth of your product or service to your customer. Doing this will move your company from just being one more supplier among many to the higher status where you become an Elite Partner. You are then considered to be a "Go To" organization — the group they turn to when they have to get things done.

TRANSACTIONAL MODE

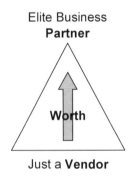

Figure 4.3

Bomel Construction has earned the reputation of being one of the best firms engaged in building concrete parking structures. When Kent Matranga, one of the owners, has an especially difficult or complex job, he knows a handful of subcontractors he can call and, without question, they will get the job done right. Those subs are Elite Business Partners in Bomel Construction's book. Every organization has a short list of contractors, employees, or companies in whom they place unequivocal trust. Those vendors have moved up to *elite* status by building worth in the transactional mode.

Sir Speedy has become an Elite Business Partner with Laguna Group. Our seminar business requires customized workbooks for each corporate client. We have to customize, produce, and ship our workbooks to locations around the world, often under tight deadlines, and they must be of the highest quality. In addition to using Sir Speedy's courier service from the local Laguna Hills center, we can log-on to their web site to access our stored documents (Sir Speedy, MyDocs™) or send new workbook documents to them via email — greatly improving our response time to our customers.

This was demonstrated recently when we had a seminar scheduled in Salvador, Brazil. Anyone who has tried to ship materials internationally knows the headaches of clearing customs and the delays that can occur. For my Brazilian seminar, Sir Speedy was able to print and produce the customized seminar workbooks at their local São Paulo facility — all from a Microsoft Word document file transferred to them using their global digital network.

Like any other successful business, we watch our bottom line, but when dealing with an Elite Business Partner such as Sir Speedy, the worth we receive far exceeds the price we pay. Sir Speedy is considered a "Go To" — they have gained Transactional Depth with us.

Sometimes your reputation as a significant "Go To" spreads industry wide. Fred spent most of his career in the movie industry, starting in the film lab and advancing into executive positions with the major studios handling post-production. His technical wizardry in the conversion of 35mm films into 70mm wide screen big productions placed him as one of the best in this field. It was part science and part art, taking a directors vision and blowing it up. Portions of the image had to be cropped in the expansion process and the critical decisions focused on what to keep and what to cut. The technical issues of color density, sharpness, and overall image quality added to the challenge of pleasing the egos of the studio executives, directors, and cinematographers. Fred was talented, hard working, and honest with all whom he interacted, earning a reputation as a dependable can-do executive.

One of the more memorable days in his career came when Barbara Striesand, one of the true divas and superstars, called him for advice. Her new film "A Star is Born" was going to be converted into a 70mm print for the wide screen theater release and her first conversion. She was concerned what the conversion process would do to her screen image and the overall quality of the film. She knew from her contacts that Fred was the person for the job based on his reputation as dependable as well as a straight shooter. Striesand did not want any "studio spin" or double talk – she wanted straight answers from someone knowledgeable. This reputation traveled with Fred as he worked with some of the biggest names in the business, always producing quality work, on time, and on budget.

This level of trust in the "transactional" components of Fred's career increased his significance, elevating him to the Elite Business Partner status. Fred is retired now, but he built a reputation that extends beyond his career. He sits on the Academy Awards voting board and is still considered an expert in his field.

Friendship Mode

This is the human element of business. People want to deal with people; it is part of our need for social interaction. It is also recognized as a quick way to progress from Phase 1 to Phase 2 in the business relationship cycle.

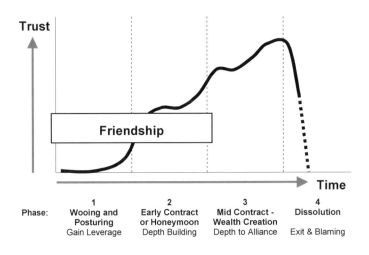

Figure 4.4

Trust is typically a given within the Friendship Mode. Insurance companies recognized this basic concept generations ago. They would hire a person and quickly get business from her or his immediate family and close friends because the new insurance agent did not have to invest a lot of time developing trust with family and friends. The pharmaceutical industry found a direct correlation between the number of field representatives and sales of drugs — the more sales reps the higher the sales. Doctors, who prescribe the medications, are positively influenced by the personal attention of a local sales representative.

The Internet B2B companies that survived the last shakeout had some common people-contact qualities — they had a toll-free phone number, an instant messaging chat facility, a responsive email system, or all three. They responded to their customers' needs for quick answers to questions or problems. Doing so increases trust. These firms also understood the basic need for human assistance and contact.

Friendship alone can take a business relationship only so far. The transactional elements must enter into the equation to move the relationship into phase 3 (wealth creation).

Friendship Depth

The goal in the Friendship Business Relationship Mode is also to get depth. The intent is to go from a contact or acquaintanceship to gaining a solid connection with the other person, and through him or her to their company.

FRIENDSHIP MODE

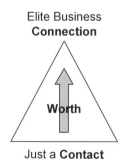

Figure 4.5

Highly successful people understand this concept — people will trust and deal with people they connect with. This is not the schmoozing or superficial stuff — it is letting people see who you really are, your values, what you can do well, and how you respond over time. Are you considered a "Go To" person — someone they will call when they need help?

Mother Theresa was one of those few who masterfully used this connection principle. Even though she was a Catholic nun in India the Hindus also revered her as a deeply religious person; her connection with people crossed religious and cultural boundaries. She had connected with some of the world's most influential and powerful people, and she could call on them for donations to her missions — and they would respond.

Friendship *Elite Connections* developed from a business transactional relationship are a rare gift. I am fortunate enough to have had such a friendship grow from a business relationship that I had with John Garcia. I first worked for John in 1984 at Bioscience Laboratories, a medical reference laboratory noted for its esoteric and cutting edge capabilities, which were used by doctors and hospitals worldwide. I was the western Area Manager and John was the VP of Marketing. Together we experienced business at a level many people only read about during business school. We went through an economic upheaval in the healthcare market place that zapped our profits; we experienced consolidations of facilities and personnel that, though prudent, were painful; eventually we transitioned the company through acquisition.

John and I got to know each other well during those times — we both got to see the other's "Go To" qualities and built our own elite connection. John has moved on to many great positions since then, and he has always kept in touch with me. Twice I went to work with him at other companies based on our "elite business partner" relationship and also in part to our growing friendship. He keeps kidding about hiring me again for a third time and making it a "Hat Trick." We both know that working together again would be a pleasure. We still keep in contact with each other - our friendship depth stronger than ever. We both consider each other "Go To" people which has moved our relationship to the business and friendship elite levels.

Getting to the significance level in either mode is a proven way to "lock in" long term relationships. Obtaining the highest levels in both ensures your legacy.

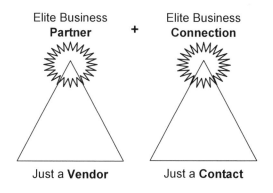

Figure 4.6

THE TRIPLE CROWN OF BUSINESS WORTH

Person

Product

Company

Handling Adversity

Ask any group of sports fans about the phrase, *Triple Crown,* and you will get a variety of responses. Some might say the phrase originated in Great Britain and applied when an English, Irish, Scottish, or Welsh national Rugby team defeated all three of its opponents in a single season. It was also given to the winner of England's three major horse races, the Two Thousand Guineas, the Derby, and the St. Leger. The phrase came across the pond to the United States when sportswriter Charles Hatton covered Gallant Fox winning the Kentucky Derby, Preakness, and Belmont in 1930.

It has been adopted by many other sports such as baseball, cycling, harness racing (one for trotters and one for pacers), softball, surfing, and more. Golfers stake a claim to the title for winning the British, U.S., and Canadian Open tournaments in a single season, a rare feat accomplished by Lee Trevino in 1971 and then by Tiger Woods in 2000. The term, *Triple Crown,* has become synonymous with winning three of something valuable.

A much more venerable use of the *Triple Crown* concept throws light on how *Worth* can be defined in business today. The definition harks back to the *Dark Ages* in Britain, to the misty, skimpily recorded centuries between the departure of the last Roman legion in A.D. 407 and the arrival of the Normans under William the Conqueror in 1066.

The myths and legends of Camelot and King Arthur are set early in the Dark Ages, a time when almost constant warfare raged. Repeated barbarian invasions by Saxons, Danes, and other warlike peoples had divided the island into a patchwork of small, mutually hostile kingdoms. Slowly — by means of warfare, diplomacy, marriage, and treachery — the dozens of petty kingdoms consolidated into just three: England, Scotland, and Wales. The great challenge of the age then became to unify the entire island.

Figure 5.1

"Only when one monarch controls the three crowns — England, Scotland, and Wales — will there be stability in the kingdom," farsighted people said. Internal peace

and the strength to deter invasion, they realized, depended on all three major entities being strong and united. Bringing the three crowns together was the key to survival.

Shifting attention to modern days, the dynastic wars of old are now the battles between companies for profits and survival. As with the old concept of keeping the three crowns healthy and united, a new model of explaining value has developed. In the equation of Price + *Worth* = Value, the *Triple Crown* concept is the Rosetta stone of translating *Worth*.

Just as the discovery of the Rosetta stone was the crucial breakthrough that led to the decipherment of Egyptian hieroglyphs after their meanings had been lost to mankind for nearly two thousand years, the *Triple Crown* represents the translation of *worth* in the value equation of business relationships. The three crowns in business are *Person, Product*, and *Company* — if each is strong and imparts *worth*, there will be stability in the business relationship.

TRIPLE CROWN OF BUSINESS WORTH

Person	Product	Company
People deal with people they trust and like	Logic and emotion of the deal	Stability and security of the relationship

Figure 5.2

Weakness in any of the three presents an opportunity for "invasion" by a competitor — or for customers to exit because they perceive degradation in the *Worth* being offered. It is the whole content or the combined effects of all these elements that create the *Worth* perception in the mind of customers—thus enhancing and reinforcing the value equation you offer.

♛ Person

The first crown in order of importance addresses the human element—the people side of business. As one world-class entrepreneur remarked, "I'd rather have a first-class team of people with a mediocre business plan than a first-class plan with a mediocre team of people."

What characteristics do first-class organizational teams bring to every business day? They bring integrity, honor, mutual respect, and a true willingness to help. They also give personal attention to the vital issue of finding and meeting the needs of individuals in ways that ensure loyalty and passion.

A case in point was the ABB Power Plant division in Toronto, Canada. As they were working to secure a nuclear power plant construction project in China, many problems faced them, the most pressing being to obtain better pricing from their suppliers. When I first started working with the management team in 1994, they wanted me to conduct seminars for their purchasing and engineering teams on "how to get tough with suppliers." After researching the problem we put together a plan that got to the core issue, but in a much more effective way.

As a result, when supplier representatives visited, something quite different from their previous practice took place. It began with the purchasing manager (PM) taking the representatives to the company cafeteria, buying them coffee or tea, and sitting and chatting for a few minutes. The PM would ask them about their business, how long they were in sales, what they liked about their work, and so on — all pleasant questions that showed a genuine interest in the individual people.

As they walked back to the office the PM would show the representatives a group of open cubicles with desks, telephones, copiers, and fax machines, and indicate that this area was for their use.

"We know you salespeople travel a lot," the PM would say, "and sometimes you need a quiet place to make a few phone calls, or catch up on paperwork. This is our way of saying you are always welcome here — even if we are not doing business with you today because we want to keep the door open for future business."

Back at the office the PM always gave the supplier an ABB annual report, and some brochures about the Power Plant division. "These will give you an idea who we are." At the end of the visit the PM would casually mention, "By the way, we have a potential project coming up for building nuclear power plants in China. I may need some help from you on this, so give it some thought and let me know if it is of interest to your company."

When the supplier came back (and they all did), they were eager to work with pricing. The ensuing process was not confrontational, and the old abusive power tactics were not used. Instead, the price negotiations were a series of candid discussions among purchasing, engineering and the supplier about how to reduce the cost of the project Respect and concern for the individual and making sure that the supplier had a fair profit were key components of each negotiation.

ABB did win the award of the power plant contract in China; it was a proud day for ABB and Canada. The materials management team felt this process enabled them to reach better deals faster than using the old abusive negotiating techniques.

Wal-Mart — noted for its operational excellence, is also noted for the personal touch. Take the concept of the store greeter who welcomes every Wal-Mart customer with a warm "Hello." This friendly greeting sets the tone for each entering customer to feel welcome and gives the feeling of a personal relationship. Interestingly, the store greeter concept was drawn from the employee suggestion box. They know that low prices might be the draw to get you in the store, but it takes a little more to keep you coming back. This is an important clue to why Wal-Mart continues to grow at a rapid rate worldwide.

We all have horror stories of a person who ruined our relationship with a company: the sales representative whose main concern was his commission or deadline, not solving or caring about your need; the service representative who made it clear that your business was not as important as his time or ego; or the telephone contact person who valued policy and procedure over common sense when handling your problem. These are examples of people who — deliberately or unknowingly — can sabotage your hard-won business relationship with a valued customer.

People want to do business with people, particularly ones they like and trust. The individual in your company who connects with another individual in the other company, adds *Worth* to the business relationship.

Person Crown Summary

People deal with people they like and trust.
The desire for human interaction and acceptance
by people that make them feel comfortable.

◆ Spend face-to-face time with your suppliers, customers and employees.

◆ Develop a consistent style and culture of doing business. Do not promote an open-door policy high on trust with employees and do the reverse with suppliers by withholding information and negotiating like a bully. Employees see the dichotomy, you cannot fool them, and this creates distrust as to the "real" organization culture.

◆ Introduce your great staff to your suppliers and customers. They are an integral part of your business and the contacts made could solidify the long-term relationship between organizations.

◆ Send handwritten thank-you notes or just keeping in touch notes. Send newspaper and magazine clippings, or links to web sites of business interest.

◆ Include pictures of your staff in proposals. Some organizations send photos of the customer support team to distant customers; it helps them put a face-with-a-name in otherwise impersonal situations.

◆ Visit or call frequently, more than just when you need business. Have a purpose, make a two-minute call to check on shipment arrival, or following-up on problem resolution makes a powerful impression.

◆ Adopt an inverted pyramid, the customer is most important, and the people who support the customer are next. Most important is to back-up this philosophy by designing organization systems and processes to support those front line people.

◆ Remember the Vidal Sassoon slogan, *"If you don't look good, we don't look good."* A marketing plan can create a perception of value in the minds of your customers, but only if it is backed by timely action from your people.

Product

Product is the sum total of everything you and your company bring to solve your customers' problems and meet their requirements. It is the goods or services you bring to the negotiating table. This is the tangible *give-to* in the relationship that hopefully enables you to serve your customers' needs better than anyone else can. A vital part of this process is getting your customers to experience your product with the same passion that you feel.

Sometimes a changing situation brings the concepts of *Product* and *Person* into conflict — with uncertain results.

Brian, an East Coast surgical equipment representative, had strong business ties with his customers. He had mastered the technical knowledge of his products and could provide details and performance specifications quickly and accurately to his customers. The products had a solid reputation for reliability and quality, and Brian strived to match that perception with his own high quality customer service.

He kept detailed records on every customer, knowing their usage and concerns, educational backgrounds, organizational charts and procedures — enabling him to provide exceptional service. He knew which customers liked to have breakfast with him at 5:00 a.m. before surgery. He knew the customers who took cigarette breaks on the roof of the hospital and at what times — often joining them even though he did not smoke.

After years of proving his expertise and worth, he decided to start his own distributorship and parlay his customer intimacy into a new business venture. He approached his current employer and demanded that they give him the product line to market through his new company. He had leverage in this negotiation because everyone knew how well he controlled his customers — to not give him the line was to walk from approximately $3 million in revenue. However, strategically the company wanted to maintain direct representation with its customers, so they had to say no to Brian's offer.

Brian resigned from his position and started his distributorship with a competitor's product. His original company worked hard to keep its established business base. They brought in experienced people to work with the customers while a new representative was being trained, and offered long-term contracts with incentives for staying. After the first year, the company was stunned. They had lost very little business.

They had expected most of the customers to switch, based on their strong identification with and loyalty to Brian. Surprisingly, the customer comments still favored Brian, but they did not have faith in his new product line. They made comments such as, "Brian is a great guy, and I want to do as much business with him as possible, but his new line just isn't as good as your product. We can't take that risk."

The customers had decided to use a product based on its quality, reputation, and performance. They valued the personal relationship and service, but in this case, not at the expense of the product issues. The transactional component is a critical part of any business relationship. Some people confuse friendship as loyalty, but it takes confidence in the product to sustain a business relationship long term.

Toyota has built a strong product reputation in its automobiles, often it is rated as the most reliable in its class and given consistently high quality marks by independent automotive groups. But recent customer surveys revealed a troubling problem with its dealer network, indicating a strong dissatisfaction with some of the sleazy and unprofessional car-sales tactics. In one survey, three out of five consumers indicated they went to another dealership out of frustration with the buying process.

Toyota knows their strong product image is holding customers for now, but they will lose customers to its competitors who are closing the gap in their product quality. Toyota understands product alone cannot keep customers satisfied in today's market. So they are in the process of raising the dealer network up to the same high standards of the rest of the organization.

Understanding how your customers use the product can provide valuable feedback. 30 years ago Arm & Hammer Baking Soda was promoted only as a cooking product, with the consumer using a portion of a teaspoon during baking. A marketing manager received feedback from consumers who used an open box to "freshen" the refrigerator by absorbing odors. This was exciting to the company because using a whole box versus only a teaspoon-at-a-time boosted sales dramatically. More customer feedback followed on how they found that dumping a box down the garbage disposal eliminated odors in the sink. Next thing you know it is dumped on carpets, added to kitty litter, used in toothpaste, and the list goes on. The product worth can also be redefined by the customer, organizations who listen closely to the users can dramatically improve a product's acceptance.

Being the actual device, service, or intangible offering a company produces, *Product Worth* is the key part of the business relationship, and it is one the customer grades every day.

Product Crown Summary

Logic and emotion of the deal.
The reasons and feelings of doing business.

◆ Discover what the customer needs from your product or service and show how it is better at those issues than the competition. This may be simplistic advice, but after the initial deal is struck suppliers often assume customers remember or do not need reassured on the original value proposition.

- Reinforce the whole "package" of your product or service. These are the support systems that are an integral part of the deal – customer service, technical support, warranty, and so on.

- Send testimonials on product or special service from other customers, 3rd party evaluations and comparisons, anything that continues to support your product's unique features and benefits.

- Spend time observing your customer using your product. Not only is your interest in their business a compliment to them, it is also a great way to learn more about their operations and gain ideas for product enhancements.

- Preview past reasons for doing business - constantly remind your customer why they originally picked your product.

- Promote quality standards that your product follows. ISO 9000, Six Sigma. If a service, list the professional group standards adopted.

- Point out your customer's past positive experiences with product or service every chance you can.

👑 Company

Your customers link you and your product with a group or organization. Business-to-business relationships start with the concept of a connection between organizations. People seek financial security and a sense of stability in long-term business relationships. The organization is viewed as supporting and perhaps outliving individuals — which has the power to instill a sense of commitment and longevity.

Sometimes innocent remarks can have a dramatic impact on a person's perception of the company's *worth* — and again the results are often uncertain.

Sally, a medical supply sales representative, built a strong customer allegiance during her eight-year career with a major healthcare company. Her customers trusted and enjoyed the professional and personal attention she brought to their business. After a two-year slow decline in her sales and commissions, Sally left for a new position.

The management team tried to keep Sally, but her mind was made up. The company then put together a *swat–team* to contact her customers and keep the remaining business until a new representative could be found.

It was no surprise that the customers expressed sadness in losing Sally as a representative. Most praised her personal service and dedication, and some even berated the management team for letting this wonderful person go. The surprise came in some of the stories and details that followed. One particularly vocal customer scolded a manager over the loss of Sally. The manager responded with a challenging question; "If you really valued Sally, why did you give her business to her competitor six months ago? The loss of sales and commissions is one of the reasons for her leaving."

"I would have given the business to that competitor a long time ago," the customer responded.

"Sally kept the business for you people. You guys can't produce my surgical kits on time. Sometimes she borrowed kits from other hospitals so we could keep doing surgeries. Other times, Sally drove up to Irvine on the weekends and put together and sterilized our kits so we could do surgery on Monday — thank goodness we had her, or you guys would have lost business a long time ago."

"We manufacture all our product in Puerto Rico," the manager said. "In fact, with the California laws against gas sterilization, we can't manufacture in Irvine. I don't know how that could be."

The customer's expression eloquently conveyed his confusion.

The manager heard similar stories from other customers. One of Sally's job responsibilities was to supply production with monthly forecasts of customer usage, but the forecasts had slipped through the cracks. At first the manager suspected that Sally had probably been innocently blaming the company for her shortcomings, while trying to make herself look good. Gradually, the manager began to see a pattern as more of the comments she had made came to light.

"I guess our production people fouled-up again. Don't worry, I'll take care of you."

"You know how those bean-counters at my company are, always trying to cut corners and expenses."

"Looks like our 'just in time' is now 'just-not-in-time."

"I can't believe they did this to you. I'll go straighten them out."

Over time her customers began losing faith in her company. The seemingly harmless criticisms, real or exaggerated, slowly eroded the customers' confidence. Eventually they placed their business elsewhere.

Company worth plays a large part in how businesspeople decide whom to do business with. The core values of the organization, and the visible systems the customers interact with, make a lasting impression. Losing confidence or not seeing the worth in the structure or systems is dangerous for long-term stability.

The organization is viewed as a collection of individuals and their culture. When we have sense of commitment to an organization, it is because we identify with its culture.

When IBM launched the PC, it had an unparalleled company image for stability and reliability. "You can't go wrong picking IBM to supply your main frame computer," data processing managers assured each other. Widely regarded as towering over all rivals, IBM easily seized control of the desktop computer market on the strength of their organization's image, a brilliantly executed automated production line, and their tradition-breaking decision to encourage third-party programs.

They had their internal problems, just as any other organization does. But IBM was legendary for presenting a united front to their customers. The internal slogan, "What's discussed inside the company, stays inside the company," kept the gossip away from people who did not want to hear it. Their sales force focused on the strengths of IBM as a cohesive organization, and effectively communicated this belief to IBM's customers.

Demand for the revolutionary new devices was far too explosive for any one company to control the market for long. Nevertheless, IBM's entry into personal computing changed the way the world conducts business in a remarkably short time.

Companies often make a solid mark in their field by developing a culture and systems that foster a memorable image. Nordstrom built its retailing success on the quality of the people it hires and the systems it provides to support them. They welcome returned merchandise and will cheerfully refund the sale, even if the product is worn or used. Keeping the customer happy and returning to their store is good for business, they know.

The result is a retailing environment conducive to having customers happily displaying license plate holders reading, "I'd rather be shopping at Nordstrom." With service levels so high, it is no surprise to find surveys indicating that many of their customers would gladly donate money to keep Nordstrom in business! This high level of support translates into booming business at their upscale stores.

Company Crown Summary

Stability and security of the relationship
Systems, structure and culture of the organization

- ◆ Introduce people from your company to corresponding departments in your supplier and customer organizations. Get your financial people to interact with their financial people, operations with operations, and so on. The direct link is better than the "middleman" negotiator to solve problems, find opportunities, and to deepen the relationship.

◆ Develop systems to expedite business communication. Phone systems, voice mail, email, interactive web pages, fax back systems – all leave an impression, make sure yours are supporting your image.

◆ Send clippings of news articles about your company, annual reports, and press releases to suppliers and customers. It keeps them attuned to your business, making their role easier.

◆ Develop a consistent culture and style; from business logo to stationary to the way you conduct business. The straight dealing (tough but fair) style of business is far better than the "slick" or overly tactical approach.

◆ Financial stability is the cornerstone of security in business. Making a profit is the best indicator that your business will be around to backup the commitments you are making. Let your suppliers and customers know of your organizations profitable history.

◆ To maintain a competitive advantage in your market, you must know the strengths and weaknesses of your organization's strategy, culture, and structure. Survey suppliers, customers and employees to validate your organization's perceptions.

◆ Graciously accept praise when your company does good things – reinforce the positive deeds back to the responsible people. Do the same to your supplier and customer organizations – write letters or emails of praise to top management when you find someone doing positive things. The praise message will filter down to the responsible person, and they will be gracious to your organization for the kudos.

♦ Develop a customer advisory group, or an executive roundtable, to gain candid feedback and direction. Design it so the group functions as a board of directors, working on real business issues.

♦ Implement a reward and recognition program with your Elite Business Partners. Structure joint retreats and activities to enhance communication and intimacy with other key people from your company.

The Triple Crown Concept goes beyond mission statements, or marketing slogans. Winning edge businesses consciously build these elements into the day-to-day functions of their organization. Each department knows how, and why they impact each of the crowns.

Figure 5.3 is a planning tool that can be used to challenge all functions of your organization to identify their unique contributions of worth to each of the crowns. If a part of the organization is not adding significant worth to any of the crowns, they might be excess baggage dragging the rest of the company down.

Solid worth in all three components creates a unified image to the business customer. Challenge your organization to become world-class in each of the components of the Triple Crown. It can keep the competition away and create a positive work environment for your employees.

TRIPLE CROWN OF BUSINESS WORTH

Person	Product	Company
People deal with people they trust and like	Logic and emotion of the deal	Stability and security of the relationship

Figure 5.3

Emerson said, "What you *do* shouts so loudly in my ears that I can't hear a word you are saying." The wisdom behind this quote has powerful implications for every business.

Handling Adversity

Johnson & Johnson had a nightmare on its hands when several customers died after ingesting cyanide-laced Tylenol. Capsules of cyanide had been inserted in a number of bottles of the nation's most popular headache remedy by a vicious extortionist. The company's response to this problem graphically demonstrates the power of the *Triple Crown of Worth*.

First, they invited Sixty Minutes to film their internal company discussions live. Considering the combative style of the Sixty Minutes News Show, it was a gutsy move. However, Johnson & Johnson wanted the public to know what the company was doing in response to the problem.

The Sixty Minutes film showed executives making decisions usually made behind closed doors. The film showed the executives agreeing to remove the suspect product from store shelves, at a high cost to the company, even though they felt sure that outside tampering was responsible.

Sixty Minutes showed the internal debate on how to improve the manufacturing and packaging process, and even the so-called experts who recommended changing the product's name.

The investment earmarked to improve the *Product* was also remarkable. Johnson & Johnson came up with tamperproof packaging, thus pioneering a new industry safety standard. The introduction of caplets to replace the tampered capsules made the product's safety visual.

The *Person* equation was approached on two fronts. The media and PR campaign giving consumers details of the problem's solution was powerfully reinforced by personal visits to the healthcare gatekeepers. The entire Johnson & Johnson sales force was used to contact every doctor and nurse available to personally explain the solution and answer questions. This remarkable personal investment enhanced the total value perception. The reintroduction of Tylenol to the market set sales records. The entire Johnson & Johnson response is a great example of the power of the *Triple Crown of Worth to* solidify business relationships even in the face of severe problems.

The lesson is that *winning edge* companies have the foresight to prepare for the inevitable disaster. Recovery and stability are linked to developing a strong Triple Crown as part of your company culture.

Here is an example of how to lose the business relationship. A German auto manufacturer had a problem with rapid acceleration in its cars. Do you remember how they dealt with the problem?

First, they emphasized the lack of *Product Worth* by denying the problem. That did not fly, so they blamed their customers, which lowered the *Person Worth*. As the pressure grew, they stonewalled the media and adopted an almost arrogant attitude, thus making *Company Worth* nonexistent. Eventually the auto manufacturer removed the car brand from the market because it had lost so much value in the customers' eyes.

A decrease in worth perception of only one of the three can spell disaster, as shown by two of the airlines that had fatal crashes in the late 1990s: ValueJet and Swissair. Remember those disasters? Fourteen months after the ValueJet crash, their lack of perceived *Company* strength forced them out of business; what remained of the company was merged into AirTran Airways. This happened even though ValueJet had strong *Person* in the form of a corps of outstanding, friendly employees.

The solid *Company* reputation, as well as *Product Worth* and *Person Worth,* that Swissair had built over the years, helped them endure the crisis. Swissair survived.

Assessing Relationship Risk:

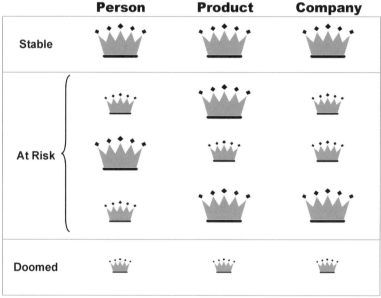

Figure 5.4

Over the years, business schools extolled the virtues of developing a strategy that focused on only one competency — low cost, or best service, or most innovative technology, and so on, implying that mastering one area would secure market dominance. This advice appears flawed in today's business-to-business environment.

An example is the copier market where one executive in the business explained that copiers actually do two things: They make copies and they break down. Manufacturers can build the fastest, sharpest, most feature-laden copier imagined, but without a top-notch service organization to keep them running, they cannot keep customers long term. Technical competence in the product without competent service and support people is like having a song in which the words and music do not match. The discord is obvious. The person buying the copier may like the features, but the person working with the copier is more interested in prompt, efficient service-people.

The group decision-making process in most organizations involves a mix of people with varied opinions and wants, and the collective group often demands excellence in all areas.

Individual Impact

Lee Iacocca took control of Chrysler when it was nearly bankrupt. He knew he had to instill confidence in his own management team, the unions, and the consumer — a daunting task considering the shape of his company and the US auto industry at the time. He became the company's spokesman — pitching the new product design, the K-car, selling the unions on quality and wage controls, and eventually paying back the federally funded loan well ahead of schedule.

He became a priceless asset to the company as the chief element of its marketing plan. Time magazine honored him with this cover — placing his head as the hood ornament on the K-car. Iacocca became the Person, Product, and Company to the marketplace.

Time Cover is reprinted with
permission of Time Inc.

Figure 5.5

Some say it was his unique talents and leadership that saved the company. He is an incredibly talented auto executive, and I think he knew people would take the leap of trust and buy Chrysler products if they believed in the company and its leader. We can learn from this example. Your organization's primary customer-contact people have a tremendous impact on the customers' *Worth* perceptions.

<u>Triple Crown Summary</u>

Building Worth perception in each of the three crowns increases:

1. Value perception

A consistent and balanced message is created by the holistic sum of the parts. The words and music are synchronized with the value proposition being offered. Creating a high value perception means that you will stand out in comparison to your competitors.

2. Relationship strength

The company's ability to outlast problems (repel invasion). Every organization has competitors trying to woo customers away — surviving problems, and the speed of recovery, are directly linked to Worth perception in all three crowns. Loyalty is the direct result of a strong Triple Crown.

3. Increased satisfaction

Contentment with the business relationship (stability in the kingdom) means that people on both sides gain feelings of *Esprit de Corp* — pride in working for and with a winner. When *Esprit de Corp* is high and runs deep, harmony in the organizational culture is evident.

WHY STRIVE FOR THE ALLIANCE MODE?

Alliance Mode

Partnership vs. Alliance

Alliance Give-Get Model

Resentment: The Deal Killer

The longevity of a one-dimensional deal is always at risk. If price is the deciding factor, someone can always undercut your price. New entrepreneurs with lower overhead or large companies willing and able to buy market share are constant competitive realities.

If it is a patented product, the patent will eventually expire. Most pharmaceutical companies face this issue at the end of a drug's patent life when generic equivalents flood the marketplace.

If it is a new technology, competitors will quickly match or exceed your breakthrough. For an example of how fast it happens and how intense it can become, look at the cell phone and its rapid pace of leapfrogging technology.

Gaining depth in the Transaction and the Friendship components can often delay the inevitable. However, without constant attention, the one-dimensional deal will shift to a better one-dimensional-competitor's deal.

Consider the example of a major telecommunications company that had contracted with a regional supplier for the installation of local fiber optic cable networks.

After a two-year uneventful relationship with the original supplier, Dave, a newly promoted purchasing manger for the telecommunications company sent out an RFP (Request for Pricing) to other local cabling contractors. He sees that he will be able to save, at minimum, five percent by switching to another cabling contractor. Dave grew up in the telephone company business; he knew that pulling copper wire is not brain surgery. After seeing the higher prices the old supplier was charging, he decided their gravy train had pulled out of the station. Dave estimated that a hundred-thousand dollars would be saved over the next two years, and confidently expected to be hailed as a hero by his organization.

At first it looked like the new contractor was working well. The installs were coming in roughly on time and looked like good work. However, after some of the new customers began complaining about significant signal (db) losses over the fiber optic circuits, Dave discovered that the contractor was using untrained laborers to install the cable. When you pull Fiber Optic cable too hard, the glass strands break. You also have to use special tools for the connectors — bad splices further degrade the signal. The complaints increased. Dave was able to spin the problems for his bosses, citing bad material, bad weather, blaming the supplier a little — and in general dodging the problems pretty well. He knew that because he picked this new contractor over one that was performing well, he had to defend them.

Little incidents started to pop up that should have been a warning, but at the time were just irritating events. At a technology office park complex, two installers had a fistfight over "whose tool was whose." The mêlée knocked over and injured a receptionist. At a major law firm the contractor's crew heckled and harassed the staff and clients so much they were asked to leave the job site and the law firm cancelled the contract on the spot. Many other issues surfaced that had never been a problem with the old supplier, and the sales and marketing people were starting to complain to Dave, saying their referral list of customers was starting to give out negative comments.

A major hospital installation went bad fast. The fiber-optic cable run went from the street to the hospital and included the second floor offices of the hospital. The contractor had used one long length of PVC coated cable to save time and costs with connectors and splices.

The building inspector red flagged the job because code called for Plenum (smoke and fire retardant) cable when crossing floors of a building. This is a major safety issue, especially in a hospital. When the contractor balked at redoing the project and declared bankruptcy, Dave had to find another supplier to take over the project. All the cable had to be scrapped because it had been pulled incorrectly, causing unacceptable breaks and signal loss. The cost of new cable including the Plenum cable ate up all the profit on the job.

The complaints from the hospital, the technology park, and other customers finally gave top management at the telecommunications company a heads-up. Dave immediately lost his job — after holding it for less than a year. No one remembered the five percent cheaper rate he got — but they would be a long time forgetting the cost overruns and the damage to the company's reputation that cost it hundreds of thousands of dollars in missed opportunities.

This is typically the worst nightmare for supplier and customer — the customer leaves the relationship for the better price, and should have stayed with what turned out to be a much better deal overall. This often happens when new people are involved who may not be aware of the history of the current supplier or deal. In this example the burden is with the supplier. They should have persisted in trying to persuade Dave and his organization from making the bad decision for the quick short-term profit.

The "dark side of the Force" can be alluring. What can the supplier do to help prevent the customer from being tempted?

Alliance Mode

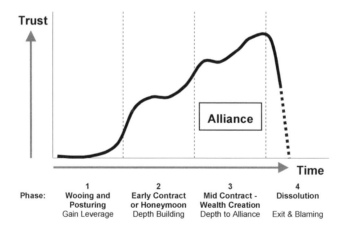

Figure 6.1

The Alliance mode is the combination of the best of Transactional and Friendship levels *plus* a mechanism for gaining additional wealth as a result of dealing with each other. It is only possible to develop this level of business in the Third Phase because trust and the value of the business deal must be high. The proper groundwork in developing trust and building worth during phases 1 and 2 enables this potential transition.

This nexus of trust and worth is called the threshold of significance.

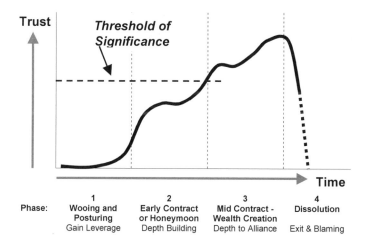

Figure 6.2

One of the distinguishing features of progressing towards the Alliance Mode is the shift from Give and Take (one-sided) negotiation style to a more balanced Give and Get style. This is a subtle but important difference in the balance of power between parties.

The Give and Take Style

Implies that one person is doing the deal (Figure 6.3), and is making all decisions as to what to give and what to take. It implies manipulation in that one person structures the deal.

Give & Take Style
1 Person Controlling

Figure 6.3

Tactics dominate this style to the point where it becomes an intense game. The negotiators can get caught up in the game and spend too much time trying to outmaneuver the other side, often forgetting that the goal *is* to structure a deal. In phase 2 and 3, this style can lower the trust between organizations.

Give and Get Style

This style (Figure 6.4) signifies a more adult or collaborative approach. *Both* sides participate in making decisions on the deal and in sharing responsibility for the outcome.

Give & Get   Give & Get
Each Person Contributing
Both Involved
Both Committed

Figure 6.4

Partnership vs. Alliance

The old partnership model was considered to be a 50/50 proposition. Each side would invest an equal amount, and they would split the resulting profits of the deal down the middle — fifty percent for each partner. History has shown that rarely does this work in the real business world. The partnership model has the highest dissolution rate when compared to other models — sole proprietor, corporation, LLC, and so on.

This happens largely because it is rare for both sides to contribute equally to the relationship. The higher contributing partner eventually develops resentment towards the partner he or she is supporting. The relationship is usually out of balance — resulting in a separation of partners.

In the Alliance mode, each side is contributing differently to the relationship, and on the surface it may not appear to be equal. But each side usually perceives a benefit from the deal that often surpasses their investment.

A McKinsey study found that 50 percent of alliance failures are due to poor strategy, and the other 50 percent are the result of poor management of the relationship. In essence they usually fail in the implementation stage — a lack of clear follow-through and not monitoring the right things.

It will take a different skill set, hard work, and a new model to structure deals that will last over time.

Alliance Give-Get Model

Let us look at how the Alliance Give Get Model is structured and what it monitors. The example is of a typical supplier/customer relationship.

1. Exchange from Supplier to Customer

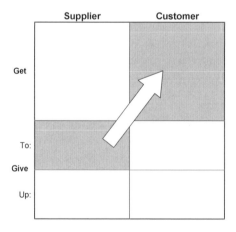

Figure 6.4

- What does the supplier *Give To* the customer in the business relationship?

    Give to is minimally the whole list of features of the supplier's product and/or service. It should also include all the items from the Triple Crown of Worth list that apply to this customer.

- What does the customer *Get* in the business relationship?

    Typically this is the reason for doing business in the first place — at the basic level it is the specific product or service features that they <u>want</u> or expect out of the business relationship. These are the things that are uniquely valuable to them, often expressed as the perceived benefits they receive in the deal. Your organization may offer many things to the markets you serve, but it is paramount to find what each customer finds of unique value — the specific things that are important to them. You cannot assume what the customer wants in this *Get* section—only they can tell you.

    Refine your customer-specific marketing plan from the complete list of your offering's benefits, narrowing it from the broad stroke approach to razor-sharp focus.

2. Customer to Supplier Exchange

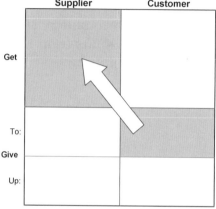

Figure 6.5

- What does the customer *Give To* the supplier in the business relationship?

  These are the things that the customer brings to the relationship that have value to the supplier. This should at a minimum be the exchange of currency for your product or service. Most customers have difficulty in developing this list beyond the money stage; it is a new way of thinking for them. This is one of the critical areas for a supplier to explore. A customer's loyalty is proportional to the commitment exhibited by items offered in the *Give To*.

- What does the supplier *Get* in the business relationship?

  Here are several possibilities:

  – Getting payment terms with better cash flow

- Rewards for hitting or beating deadlines
- Gaining knowledge about the customer's operations and systems — know-how that can teach you new methods or help you improve your operations
- Obtaining access to your customer's end customers — leading to learning how and where your product fits — which in turn gives your organization real time research and new product ideas and improvements in existing ones.

A growing area of value to both suppliers and customers is tapping into each other's knowledge databases. Each side gains access to vital information that is not readily available to them.

Knowledge Database

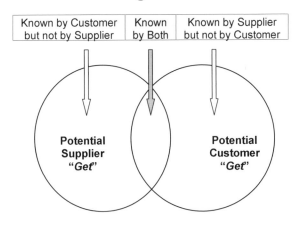

Figure 6.6

Manufacturing organizations are finding that suppliers are a growing source of technology advancements. Consider the personal computer. IBM launched the PC with the intention of driving the market with its hardware model. The IBM alliances with Intel and Microsoft quickly indicated that the suppliers were the driving force in technology innovations. IBM prospered in the early years of the PC explosion via its access to Intel and Microsoft knowledge.

Often this link in information goes beyond just two partners. Medical device-maker Baxter is working with software giant Microsoft and networking company Cisco Systems to develop an Internet-connected home kidney dialysis machine. This alliance and the sharing of each company's Knowledge Database will allow healthcare professionals to remotely monitor the patient and adjust treatment protocols.

3. What do both sides *Give Up* in the process of doing business together?

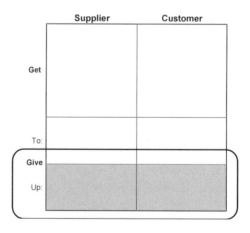

Figure 6.7

This is the investment each side makes to the business relationship. Included are the costs directly and indirectly associated with the transactions — time, money, and energy — plus the impact the investment has on other relationships. Each side should recognize the contributions and respect the others time away from other customers and/or suppliers.

Structure of a Joint Venture

Another example of the Alliance Give-Get Model is the recent venture between Mobil and Taco Bell to sell the Taco Bell fast food in the Mobil convenience stores. Each organization had options: Mobil considered developing or licensing its own private label food items, and Taco Bell considered building or franchising more stores in the marketplace. The goal was to be able to create more wealth in a combined venture than the other options could. In looking at the model (Figure 6.8) you can see what each side invested:

Give To   Both companies contributed marketing dollars, training, and their unique talents. Mobil has the best run C-stores and systems, including fast credit card payment options to combine fuel and food purchases. Taco Bell has a great brand image and the know-how to produce top quality food items in the Mobil C-stores.

Give Up   Both companies invested time and resources that could be spent on other projects — a serious commitment from both sides. Mobil gave up valuable floor and window space for the venture and Taco Bell risked anger from the owners of its regular franchise stores, who might feel the venture would reduce their business.

Together each side understood the investment and commitment, gaining respect and profits as a result.

	Taco Bell	**Mobil**
Get	• New customers • Brand exposure • New geographic locations without real estate investment • Media coverage and Mobil promotion	• Incremental revenue – product sales and floor space rental • Brand name connection with Mobil F^3 core customers. • Increased media exposure • New customers
To:	• Food storage and preparation systems • Access to Taco Bell core customer (young adult) • Training • Marketing $	• Resources – corporate and regional • Training of store personnel • Access to Mobil F^3 core customers • Marketing $
Give **Up:**	• Siphon business from franchise stores (risk) • Time, resources, cash flow – to invest in other projects	• Floor and window space • Private brand food items • Time, resources, cash flow – to invest in other projects

Figure 6.8

Often a result of these Alliance Give Get Model discussions is that both sides learn that the return was larger than the investment. They actually felt as if they got more out of the deal than they put into it — that is called creating wealth for both. The relationship is harder to break up when both sides feel that the deal they have now will be hard to beat by a new competitor offering just a superficial one-dimensional gain.

Resentment—the Deal Killer

Over time, if one side feels they are contributing more to the relationship than the other side— resentment can develop. This is one of the biggest business relationship deal killers. Constantly working through the Alliance Give Get Model can help identify the weak areas in the relationship, possibly preventing the cascade from resentment to exit.

An example of this was a pharmaceutical sales representative in Upstate NY, selling anti-hypertensive medication. One of his largest potential customers, a big cardiology group, was producing zero sales, even after two years of intensive effort. The sales rep visited the office twice a month, delivering free samples, giving away note pads, pens, patient education books — all the marketing materials at his disposal to gain favor from the office staff. He invited the doctors to lunch, brought doughnuts into the office, and invited the doctors to his company sponsored education symposiums — all the personal efforts he could imagine, yet to no avail.

After learning of this tool at one of my seminars, he knew he had to get his worth recognized by the doctors or he had to fire them as customers. He was agonizing over this. He told me "they are my biggest doctor group, I have to keep visiting them."

"How much business are you getting from them now?" I asked.

"Zero", he said.

"And how much business will you lose if you quit calling on them?"

He finally got the point, so he scheduled an appointment with the doctors and explained that after two years of efforts, and all the *Give To* things he did for them — he felt he must not be offering anything of value to them, and he was not gaining anything out of the relationship (his *Get*).

	Sales Representative	Customer
Get		
To: **Give**	• R_x samples • Education symposiums • Note pads, pens, post-its • Patient Education Booklets • Lunches, donuts for office • Other marketing materials	
Up:	• Time away from other customers • Responsibilities and duties of territory management • Time away from family	

Figure 6.9

He noted that his territory was large and he needed to invest his selling time in other doctor groups, so this was going to be his last visit and he wanted to say good-bye personally to them. It was very quiet for a few minutes, finally one of the senior physicians spoke and he said, "I feel embarrassed that we aren't prescribing any of your products. They are very good drugs, and you are well respected by all of us and the office staff, I just assumed that you must be getting a lot of business from us by the amount of time I've seen you here."

The doctor went on to offer to take the sales rep with him on grand rounds the next day at the hospital and introduce him to his other colleagues and to help him sell more of his products. Sales of that anti-hypertensive drug tripled in the representative's territory in the next few months; he attributes the spike in sales to having the courage to use the Alliance Give Get Model to reshape the relationship with those doctors.

TRIED AND TRUE
STRATEGIES AND TACTICS
THOSE THAT WORK AND SOME THAT
SHOULD GO AWAY

The Relationship/Issue
  Quadrants

Challenging Standard
  Practices

Punishment vs. Reward

Bracketing Solutions

Counter-Productive Tactics

The performance bar has been raised today, both in business and in sports. Both require significantly better strategy and enhanced skill levels of the participants. Consider what is now required of athletes in most sports compared to a decade ago. Whether in football, baseball, skating, gymnastics, golf, or you-name-it, today's professional athletes train more, understand strategy better, and are more systematic in approaching their sports. The level of skill and stamina that worked years ago often is woefully inadequate against the world-class competitors they face today.

The same can be said for present-day contract negotiators in business — their skill set has changed and the performance expectations are significantly greater today. The traditional roles of the purchasing manager being a tough and bluff buyer; or the vendor's representative portrayed as a handshaking, joke-telling, slick talker are becoming dated.

Those old-time roles are fast losing significance in the shift toward managing the relationship between organizations. This shift requires a critical reexamination of the traditional negotiation toolbox of tactics to develop new tactics able to perform this new task.

There are a lot of ethical tactics available when negotiating a business deal. One of the critical decisions impacting your strategy is how to balance the short vs. the long view in the relationship. Negotiation gambits that work for you while negotiating a one-shot deal, like the purchase of your car, may not transfer effectively into a long-term business relationship. You can use an aggressive strategy and tactics to get a yes once, but can you get the second, third, or fourth yes with those methods? The real core of repeat business is *continued* trust, and the tactics should support that goal not undermine it.

Negotiation strategy in long-term business relationship is fluid. It is not a single event, but a continuing series of negotiations that shape the relationship. Traditional roles of buyer and seller start to blur and, depending on the particular issue, you can be in either role or both during the same negotiation.

The Relationship/Issue Quadrants

The development of a cohesive strategy starts with an examination of the end goal of your organization. Consider the organizational interests around two areas:

How important is the <u>issue</u> outcome to the organization?

How important is the <u>relationship</u> outcome to the organization?

Strategy options are demonstrated in the chart below:

ISSUE IMPORTANCE

	High	Low
High	**I** *Strategy:* **Collaboration** to cultivate TRUST and WORTH — Phase 3 typical	**II** *Strategy:* **Co-operation** to cultivate GIVE awareness — Phase 2 typical
Low	**III** *Strategy:* **Competitive** to cultivate GET awareness — Phase 1 typical	**IV** Why waste time?

RELATIONSHIP IMPORTANCE

Figure 7.1

I. High Relationship — High Issue

If both the issue and relationship outcome rank high in importance, the strategic approach is collaboration. The cultivation of trust and worth will enhance the openness and shift to solutions that follow the Alliance Give-Get Model. The strategies support each organization's interdependent and mutually supportive climate. The problem solving process is the predominate focus.

II. High Relationship — Low Issue

If the relationship outcome is high and the issue outcome is ranked low, the strategic approach is cooperation. Maintaining a high relationship level is the primary goal. The minor-issue negotiation and associated concessions are given to promote an in-kind response later. Generating an awareness of the importance of contributing to each other (the GIVE TO in the Alliance Give-Get Model) should cultivate reciprocation later.

III. Low Relationship — High Issue

If the relationship importance is low and the issue importance is high, the strategic approach is competitive. Maintaining a value perception of the issues and concessions is the primary goal. Generating an awareness of the need for mutual benefit in the deal (the *Get* in the Alliance Give-Get Model) should lead to respect and enhance the trust levels in the relationship. In the end, shifting focus to the relationship will lower the competitive temperament.

IV. Low Relationship — Low Issue

If the relationship importance is low and the issue importance is also low, the strategic approach becomes moot. This calls into question why there is an investment of time, energy, and resources in the deal.

In any worthwhile negotiation, your choice of strategy and tactics should promote a move toward Quadrant I. This will ultimately focus both sides on the high impact negotiation items, optimizing return on investment in the relationship.

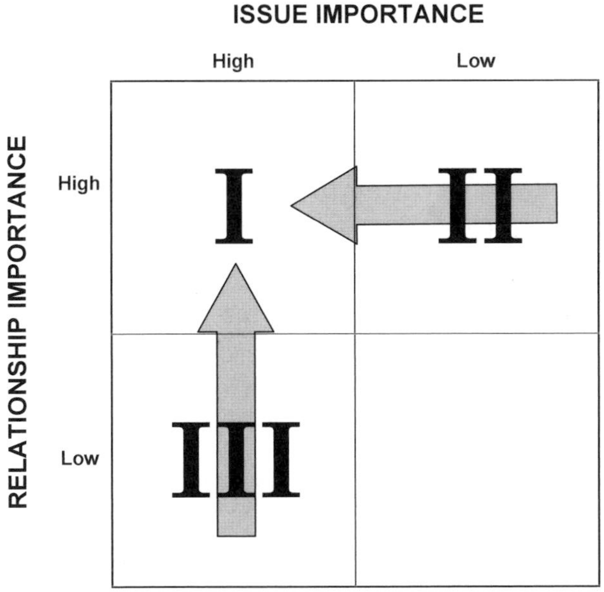

ISSUE IMPORTANCE

Figure 7.2

The next step is matching appropriate tactics and attitude to the strategy selected. Since outdated or ineffective methods can undermine the best-planned strategy, carefully question the past practices and tactics in your organization.

What are the areas you should challenge in your current negotiation portfolio?

Challenging Standard Practices

Sometimes past practices and local traditions develop into the cultural fabric that makes business dealing civil and personally highly satisfying. In the Middle East, the serving of strong coffee before and during deal negotiations is customary; Europe has its traditions of shaking hands, hugging or even kissing of the cheeks; Japan makes a ceremony of bowing to show respect and a ritual of exchanging business cards. I hope none of these charming practices that smooth the way for both parties ever disappear from the business landscape.

Other practices now come under scrutiny, some whose time has perhaps passed. These are sometimes defined as standard practices that are now presenting ethical dilemmas.

An example is a practice called *gazumping* in the UK and Australia. Although legal under English law, gazumping borders on swindle. Here is how it works: a property owner agrees to sell to the buyer for an agreed upon price. The buyer gets busy on organizing the necessary paperwork to finalize the deal and present the formal contract — a process that often takes weeks or months. It does not work this way in the US, where accepting an offer creates a binding contact, but under English law the seller is not bound to the deal until the formal contracts are exchanged. This enables the seller to renege on the first buyer's deal by accepting a better offer from a second buyer who, by having quicker access to cash, can *gazump* the first buyer. The seller can switch allegiance to a second buyer even after giving his promise to accept the first deal.

This practice obviously is a boon to the seller, but it comes close to being disreputable from the first buyer's standpoint. Local customs like this are hard to change since it is so deeply engrained in the real estate market's accepted practices. Just because something was standard practice over the years may not make it acceptable in today's business climate.

Another example is the recording industry, which is currently (in 2001) under fire for some of its standard practices in contracts with artists. The French music company Vivendi Universal has lawsuits from Don Henley and Courtney Love. The Dixie Chicks are suing Sony Corporation, and the California Senate is launching hearings on the record business practices.

There are always two sides to an argument, but the media has received very little comment from the recording industry compared to the many examples from the recording artists. The allegations surfacing get to the heart of the industry's alleged unconscionable contracts and corrupt accounting practices that artists claim hide profits and bilk them out of their earnings. Young entry-level artists, who feel that they have no bargaining power, are required to sign a standard industry contract that is presented as being nonnegotiable.

Here is what the Dixie Chicks' lawsuit alleges: the contract is so one-sided that even if they catch Sony failing to pay proper royalties, they still cannot break the contract. In fact, they must sue at their own cost to get a judgment against the company, and if successful the company still has thirty days to pay without any breach occurring.

Record companies have been known to stall payments to artists for years under this kind of contract. As a result, artists often spend more time investigating their recording company's breach of trust than in recording music. The artists expected the companies to live up to their word, and are angry to learn that not doing so is considered standard practice in the recording business.

The movie business is infamous for similar shenanigans. The studio would structure an actor or director's contract to contain a piece of the profit, and write the deal as a percent of the net profit on the movie. They did not share with the talent that the standard industry practice was to load all the expenses they could find into that project so it would show a loss or break even. No net profit, no bonus paid under the contract. The accounting games they played did border on the unethical, but the defense to this swindle was, "It's standard practice." No wonder the experienced movie people went for percent of the gross, or just for higher fees.

"That's the way we always do it," or "Those are our standard terms," are ways in which organizations hide behind a mantle of tradition while attempting to make their swindles respectable. This concept of group consensus is fraught with danger.

"If everybody else decides to jump off the bridge, that still doesn't make it the smart thing to do," my mother often told me. Personal leadership against a consensus opinion is the catalyst for progress in negotiation values and ethics. Remember the *end game* is to develop trust during the relationship. Challenge the outdated standard practices in your industry.

Punishment vs. Reward

The contracts manager for a northeastern state had the responsibility to award fuel concessions for its toll road system. He approached the process as a year-to-year bid and award process, leveraging the major oil companies against each other. The only thing he was interested in was the lowest price; he stated that the three most important things in getting this business were "Price, *price*, and **price**." The oil companies would get signage along the toll way at each station, but would have to sell gasoline at a severe loss to do so.

The state's contracts manager was incredibly arrogant. If you were unfortunate enough to represent the oil company awarded the contract, you ended up in therapy as a result of the demeaning process of dealing with this character. The contract had numerous penalty clauses, all favoring the state, that were enforced ruthlessly. For years, the oil companies competed with each other like animals to get this business, all justifying it in the name of increasing market share.

One year, an oil company decided not to respond to the bid. They decided to pass on the second year and then on the third — realizing the fight to get the contract and the losses incurred were just not worth it. After the bid closed, the oil company that had not bid for three years got a phone call from the state treasurer's office inquiring why they had not responded to the bid.

The oil executive who took the call responded politely. He explained that his company was shifting strategic focus toward building service-station value by investing in things such as better lighting, faster pumps, better fuel additives, and additional convenience stores inside their retail stations. The oil man added that the losses incurred with the state toll way contract did not make sense any more.

"Well, I have an interesting dilemma," the state treasurer said. "This year, no oil company responded to our RFP (request for pricing). I've never seen anything quite like this, and it puts me in a rather embarrassing situation. We will run out of gas at the toll way stations in three weeks if I can't find a vendor." He gave a nervous little laugh.

"Can I come down and talk to you guys — you know — to see what it would take to get you to sell us some fuel?"

The oil company executive could not talk for a few seconds because his lips were stretched from ear to ear with the biggest grin you have ever seen.

"Well, come on down — I'm sure we can work *something* out," each word dripping with glee and comeuppance! You can imagine how much they enjoyed having the tables turned. They did not sell any gasoline to the state again that year, but they did enjoy making them grovel for a while.

This scenario has been repeated to varying degrees in many industries, but the underlying theme is consistent — more and more suppliers are not selling just on price. When market prices gravitate downward, mostly from buyers demanding price only, it usually results in the better companies exiting first.

The players left in those markets will go out of business eventually, it is a matter of who can outlast whom. Only after one or two suppliers go into bankruptcy do the rest of the competitors seem to wake up and take notice. Suddenly they see what a dangerous mixture has been brewed: nasty people to deal with, punitive contract terms — and all for no profit. Creating an environment where contract winners feel like losers because they end up getting punished by the deal means that eventually the buyers will reap what they sow.

Leverage in a deal can work to move it along to closure. But the wrong kind of leverage works against fostering a long-term relationship. There is a shift away from the negative or punishment only type procurement processes.

Reward

On January 17, 1994 the California Northridge 6.7 magnitude earthquake damaged more than 25,000 buildings, closed 11 major roads, killed 57 people and injured 9,000 more. The economic loss was estimated to be more than $8 billion.

The quake smashed the Santa Monica Freeway — a vital east-west artery in the Los Angeles area. Until the quake, it had been the busiest freeway in America; and its quick rebuilding was essential to commerce in Southern California. The initial Caltrans estimates of 12 to 18 months to rebuild the damaged roads were too long for the civic and business leaders.

A revised six month's flat-out, no-holds-barred program was initiated with funding from both federal and state governments. An estimated $1 million was lost to the local economy each day the freeway system was down, in addition to the disruption in the everyday lives of the people living in the area. This was a project earmarked for high importance, and the political leaders had the incentive to move things along quickly on the bidding and construction projects.

The Caltrans employees hand delivered the cartons of plans and specifications to the five qualified contractors vying for the project, committing to evaluate the bids and award the contract — on the same day. Initially Brutoco Engineering and Construction won at $20 Million with a 100-day completion date. Brutoco withdrew its bid after they discovered an error. C.C. Meyers was the second lowest bidder at $14.9 Million but with a 140-day completion timetable. Caltrans awarded the bid to Meyer's company with an unusual incentive: a $200,000 bonus for each day the freeway was completed ahead of schedule, and a similar penalty for each day late.

Meyers took some calculated risks to make it work. He started work while the plans were in peer review at Caltrans; if they failed, he would have to start work all over. He had to use more steel and labor than he originally planned on, thus increasing his days. To counterbalance, he used expensive but fast drying concrete designed for airport runways, cutting curing time to two days from ten. His crews worked around the clock and he rewarded them with cash incentives, $100 dinner gift certificates, and a piece of his bonus.

Bottom line: Meyers completed the project ahead of schedule, earning a $13.8 million bonus. Caltrans basked in universal praise for getting a freeway project scheduled for 18 months completed in just 66 days!

This has become a model of an effective incentive based system in the construction industry. Global trend is the shift toward contract rewards based on exceeding goals in quality, on time delivery, and process improvement.

Bracketing Solutions

Time and energy invested in a deal that has no chance of reaching agreement is one of the biggest sins in business negotiating. Time is money, and the resources consumed in trying to finalize acquisitions, mergers, and even transactional contracts sometimes eat up any potential profits.

Early mechanisms for testing the waters — to see if an agreement is possible — are coming into play. The old RFP gave the purchasing agent a ballpark price figure for products they were unfamiliar with — useful for getting a reality check to see if their budget or project costs were in line.

Unfortunately, the supplier often did not have a similar mechanism to see if he was even on the same planet as the buyer when it came to expected price. Some of the old squeeze tactics that one-sided negotiators used would keep the other person constantly adjusting their offer. By making statements like, "You've got to do better than that," or "Go sharpen your pencil," they would keep their position a secret and manipulate the other side into constantly changing their position to the buyer's advantage.

The attempt by British media mogul, Robert Maxwell, to purchase the Australian Fairfax newspaper chain provides a story that gets to the heart of this issue. Maxwell was negotiating with the newspapers' owner, Warwick Fairfax, and the deal was going nowhere. It appeared to be a deadlock and each side wondered if it was worth putting any more effort and time into the negotiation. Maxwell suggested that Fairfax write the absolute minimum price he would accept on a piece of paper, and he, Maxwell, would write the absolute maximum he would pay on another piece of paper. The two pieces of paper were given to a neutral third party who looked at the numbers and then destroyed the papers, never revealing the amounts on either piece. The third party's function was simply to indicate whether a deal was possible. The negotiations were halted because the mediator saw no zone of settlement — the absolute maximum Maxwell would pay was below the absolute minimum Fairfax would accept. This saved each side considerable time and resources by not continuing to negotiate an impossible deal.

Setting the Bracket

This concept is called *Setting the Brackets*. Each party displays the min and max of the deal, showing if there is a true *Zone of Settlement,* an area where price agreement could be reached. Here is a simple example of this concept. A developer has a commercial property for sale, advertised at $600,000. A buyer places an offer for the property at $560,000. The bracket is now set.

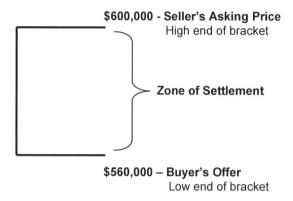

Figure 7.3

The seller knows that the absolute minimum he can expect is $560,000 — giving him the information he needs to decide if he should even continue negotiating. The buyer knows going in that the maximum he can expect to pay is $600,000. If there is an agreement reached, it is expected to fall between those two numbers, that is, within the price range bracket.

This tool works best when each side has developed trust; and fair and reasonable viewpoints are negotiated. A key caveat: employing an aggressive style of bracketing can lead to disaster.

In the late 1990s, a major chemical company wanted to buy a small producer of a specialty compound. This patented compound was a critical component in one of the larger company's most important products. They had a good relationship with the small company, but to protect and improve their profit margins they decided to acquire it.

The finance team had a very good working knowledge of the small company and they calculated the buy value at $9 million, with an $11 million high side target. Unfortunately the negotiator working the deal decided to lowball the opening offer at only $4 million.

"You can always come up in the offer, but if you start too high you will leave money on the table," was his underlying reasoning. This was wisdom left over from the old days, but a bad choice of strategy in this situation. The small company was so offended by the low initial offer that they broke off discussions.

A few weeks later, First Boston contacted the large chemical company to let them know they were handling the sale, and were sending out solicitations to the major chemical company's competitors. Now opening offers would be considered at $20 million. A bidding war ensued and the final sale price to the major chemical company was approximately $27 million!

A greedy stance in setting the bracket's opening offer position cost the major chemical company millions. A cautionary tale worth remembering in today's more enlightened business environment.

Most savvy business negotiators now try to establish brackets as soon as possible in the negotiation. The subsequent discussions focus on finding solutions to the gap, not jockeying for position. Each side is involved and committed in the process. This concept readily applies to price issues, but it is growing in use with other contract terms and negotiation issues. Some of the emerging contract issues include: more favorable terms for payments or receivables, intellectual property rights and protections clauses, non-disclosure and non-compete clauses, and the timing of each. Using the *bracket tool* sets up the mechanism to reach agreement vs. haggling over each side's position on every issue.

Counter Productive Tactics

Let's talk about a group of tactics whose time to be thrown into the trash bin of history has come. They are outdated, transparently gimmicky, and weaken or destroy long-term trust and relationships.

Good Cop, Bad Cop

Hollywood created the screen image of two police officers interrogating a crime suspect, each playing a role. The bad cop is mean and nasty to the suspect. Then the good cop takes over, offers the suspect coffee and cigarettes, and speaks in friendly tones. Obviously the suspect prefers to deal with the good cop, and not be punished by the bad cop.

If given a fresh twist, this stock scene can still make good cinema, but it is not a viable strategy in long-term business relationship negotiations. It is a dated and manipulative approach that can severely damage trust between organizations. It is also bad policy to portray an individual from your organization as a bad person; it could hurt your overall credibility.

Grinders

People who love to use time limits as a weapon are grinders. They purposely stall in the negotiations, placing time stress on the other side. They play for time on the smallest of issues, hoping to trick the other person into making-up concessions to end the torture. Often the grinders push decisions up to and sometimes beyond deadlines, paying no attention to what consequences such callous behavior imposed on the other side. The old school egocentric negotiators loved playing this power game, whose message was, "My time is important but yours is not." This not only is bad manners, it can create the image of unprofessional behavior.

Rudeness and Power Games

People who enjoyed the power of negotiating more than making good agreements used to engage in a variety of games. They would provide shorter chairs for the other side to give them a height advantage, supposedly intimidating the opponents. They would arrange the room so they would sit with their back to the window, making the other person squint into bright sunlight. Some would keep the other side waiting in the office lobby for long periods; others would pretend anger, and use screaming sessions to rattle the other person's composure.

Hitler sometimes carried this a stage further by chewing on the carpet while screaming and frothing at the mouth. He tried this on the Swiss ambassador to enforce his demand that armed German troops should be permitted to pass through the Alps to Italy. In spite of this unnerving demonstration by an apparent madman who could destroy his country, the ambassador held firm. He reminded Hitler that his country was prepared at a moment's notice to blow up the tunnels through the Alps, thus making swift movements by rail impossible. As neutrality required, unarmed German troops were allowed to pass through Switzerland, but their equipment went on separate trains.

Other outdated power ploys include: staging phone calls or interruptions by their assistant at pre-planned intervals, or doing paper work while the other person speaks. All these are head games played on the opponents with the sole intent of gaining advantage in the negotiation. Top executives who have real power do not behave like this. This old school approach never did much good and definitely is viewed as unprofessional and childish behavior today.

Deception

Perhaps all the books published in the 1990's that compare business strategy to war strategy have refueled interest in this area. There are a variety of ploys that fall into the deception category — verbal promises made (not in writing) with no intention of keeping them, delays to ask nonexistent higher authority for approval, and faux competitors. Beside the integrity issue, a danger to trust in the relationship exists when the deception is discovered. If it was a war tactic, the rationalization was no one cared about the deception — hence the expression "all's fair in love and war."

But if you plan to stay in business or want to develop long-term relationships, employing deception is dangerous. There is an expression that compares deception to an overflowing septic tank, it will become noticeable to all and is very nasty to clean up.

Long-term business relationships break down when too much time is spent planning the tactical approach to the negotiation vs. implementing the negotiation and solutions. Failure to focus on the big picture is the common mistake.

TRUST IN GOD — VERIFY ALL OTHERS

Contract Basics

Validation

Entropy and Deal Unwinding

Decision Makers

Implementation Plan

"A verbal contract isn't worth the paper it's written on," film producer Samuel Goldwyn said with unintentional Yogi-Berra wit. With that truth in mind, the best contract advice that can be given is, "Put it in writing."

A contract is the written record of the promises made by each side, including how the relationship started, how it is to be conducted, and what happens when it ends.

Contract Basics

The origins of most of the contract law in the United States are traceable to two sources: English common law developed by English royal courts between 1500 and 1800, and the combination of Roman law and Aristotelian personality theory worked out by Spanish scholars in the sixteenth century. Our law of contracts includes centuries of developing theory and culture, hundreds of rules, and many thousands of cases in which these rules have been applied and explicated. As with engineering or medicine, the profession of law is constantly evolving as each generation builds on the existing knowledge base.

Current contract law is further complicated by being the creature of each state, and the states may differ. To most lay people, this is confusing enough, but the legal profession adds the unique legalese of contracts as an additional layer of complexity and intimidation. Consider this story:

> One day in a Contract Law class, a Professor asked one of his better students, "Now, if you were to give someone an orange, how would you go about it?"
>
> The student replied, "Here's an orange."
>
> The professor was livid. "No! No! Think like a lawyer!" he shouted.
>
> "Okay." The student then recited, "I'd tell him, 'I hereby give and convey to you all and singular, my estate and interests, rights, claim, title, claim and advantages of and in, said orange, together with all its rind, juice, pulp and seeds, and all rights and advantages with full power to bite, cut, freeze and otherwise eat, the same, or give the same away with and without the pulp, juice, rind and seeds, anything herein before or hereinafter in any deed, or deeds, instruments of whatever nature or kind whatsoever to the contrary notwithstanding..."

"Now that's language you can bill for," the professor said.

As with any other profession, law requires specific language and structure to make a contract valid and defensible. Until the day that contracts are written in layman's language, always seek counsel from attorneys who are well versed in the contract law of the states involved.

If you get right down to the core of the agreement between two business organizations, the purpose of a contract is to insure that:

1. The vendor gets paid.

2. The buyer gets the product or service as promised.

Additional items are added to this nucleus, to include issues that have become important to either side over time. The seller, once sued for nonperformance because he could not deliver as a result of a flood that wiped out his plant, now wants to include a force majeure (acts of God, uncontrollable event) clause in all contracts. The buyer, who once experienced excessive construction delays in building a new facility, now wants performance clauses and strict deadlines in their contracts. Past experiences of the organizations and individuals shape their perspective towards contracts.

> *"A man who has burned his mouth with hot milk blows on his yogurt"*
>
> ——Turkish proverb

Most business contracts now contain provisions that attempt to limit the issues that can arise in a dispute. Some of the common provisions are:

- Length of the agreement

- Terms and conditions of payment

- Specification of goods or services provided

- Protection of the trade secrets and intellectual property of each party

- If a dispute arises, the method of resolution is frequently specified, which may be binding arbitration. If so, an arbitration organization such as the American Arbitration Association should be specified along with the state law that will govern, who will pay the arbitration costs, and so on.

The goal of a contract should *not* be to hide behind the law. By writing contract language that is so onerous and unfair, you increase the chances that it will be overturned if contested, especially if the other side has little or no leverage. You can negotiate a deal where one side can cancel and the other cannot, but unless you have a very good business reason, it may be overturned in some states. Why risk the relationship with dubious or heavy-handed language? Structure a good balanced contract; be on the right side of it, and your relationship will prosper.

The basic contract protects each party's interest, but increasing practices are to expand the agreement into a living roadmap to keep the relationship on track. Two particular areas to focus on are:

- executing the agreed upon contract as intended

- and keeping the deal from unraveling over time

Validation

In the 1970s urban legends grew about how rock bands sometimes put outlandish items into their contracts. *"No brown M & M's"* is my favorite. In the actual performance contract of the rock group Van Halen, one of the clauses stated, "In the dressing room there is to be a bowl of M & M's with all the brown M & M's removed." On the surface this might seem odd, or even crazy. Why would a rock band ask for that item in the contract?

To understand the world of touring bands, you have to appreciate the people who transport and set up the equipment — the roadies. They often have a short time to prepare the arena for the complex light, sound, and even pyrotechnic equipment.

The electrical and physical requirements are spelled out in detail in the contract, which the local venue must prepare to enable the show to go on. The Van Halen group's tour often took them to small markets that often were not accustomed to elaborate productions. The M & M clause was buried amid the specifications of wiring and structural details, items linked to the safety of all involved.

When the crew arrived at the arena for the preinspection, guess the first thing they will check.

Right, the bowl of M & M's. If the arena management is thorough, they will have the bowl of M & M's — sans brown ones — on display in the dressing room to indicate to the inspection crew that the other electrical and physical elements are also probably done to specification. They will check the systems and set-up because they are professionals, but not with the same sense of urgency if the telltale bowl of M & M's was missing or incorrectly done.

This is a unique example of placing verification items into contract language that guides and/or doublechecks trust in the relationship. I am not recommending that you put the M&M clause in your contracts, but the concept of following up on the signed contract terms is vital for all long-term relationships. This helps prevent the common fatal breach: *the deal that is signed is not the deal that is executed.* Whether by omission or commission, not checking or verifying contract details and proper execution risks profit and possibly the long-term relationship.

Entropy and Deal Unwinding

A force in nature causes things to become disorganized and chaotic. One of the fundamental laws of physics states that the entire universe is decaying. All things deep down at the particle level are naturally slowing down and drifting apart. The scientific term is *entropy*. Business relationships are also impacted by this phenomenon. Unless energy (work) is applied to the system, entropy moves the relationship toward decay and termination.

Some management experts believe that if people are given a choice between hard work or slacking off, they will most likely chose to slack off. A more common problem is that many companies give greater attention to gaining deals than to maintaining them. Given this natural force toward minimum energy and the drifting apart of the physical universe, it is safe to conclude that entropy applies to any business relationship. Left alone, the relationship will decay.

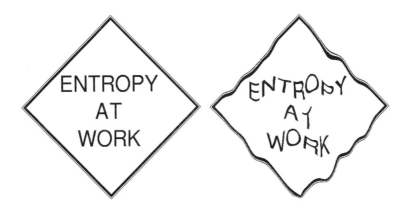

Figure 8.1

Those with an understanding of the Second Law of Thermodynamics will appreciate the oxymoron in the phrase "Entropy at Work."

In Chapter 3, I related the success story of a contract between the American Hospital Supply Corporation (AHSC) and the Medical center on the JIT stocking program. Sadly, three years after its inception, the contract was canceled and the Medical center went back to the old way of managing their own supplies and logistics.

One of the causes originated with the new management negotiation team for the Medical center; they wanted more than the original 30/70 split. They wanted it to be a 40/60 split of the $1 savings — a deal breaker for AHSC.

It was a shame because the hospital lost more than the profit; it also lost the revenue from the exam and treatment rooms that now had to be reclaimed. This is good example of new team of negotiators haggling over an additional 10 percent concession, but forgetting why the deal was done in the first place.

Both sides share some blame in the breakup of the deal, but each could have worked on the contract language or structure that would have protected their interests. The most glaring factor was not developing a transition team that would manage the deal over time. People who negotiate new venture contracts or acquisitions rarely stick around long; they move on to do other deals. Some organizations develop contract renewal or maintenance teams to fill this void. New practices entail the original negotiators writing *non-binding agreement understanding* documents. These documents plot milestone assessment points during the contract to guide the new teams through the expected targets. At minimum, each side agrees to revisit the contract and its progress on a specific timetable.

Decision Makers

Monitoring the key people in any business deal will help you gauge the positive or negative trends going on in your relationship. The support and commitment to the deal of the key people is critical to long-term success. These decision makers will increase in both number and political savvy in proportion to the size of their organization.

For example, a supplier dealing with a small accounting firm will have no problem tracking the decision makers; they are probably in one office and all visible just by scanning the room. The supplier can easily receive direct feedback from the decision makers and users of the product; often they are one in the same.

Compare that small firm to a multinational accounting/consulting organization and the number of people and the management layers of the organization increase by astronomical proportions. This presents a challenge to the supplier in identifying who uses the product and who are the real decision makers. In these large complex organizations there are regional and corporate offices, some of the decisions are centralized and others are decentralized. Often the person negotiating the deal is a professional negotiator with no direct ties to or use for the supplier's product. This person's goal is to unemotionally hammer out a good deal for their side.

There are also subtle but important differences in *keeping* the business vs. *getting* the business as it relates to group dynamics. In Phase 2 and 3 of the relationship, the strategy shifts toward defending your growing worth and significance. Competitors will undermine the relationship if they can. Like the invading armies of old England, they look for a weakness to exploit. A strong Triple Crown is the best foundation for defense if all the decision makers believe in it.

The security of your deal and of the business relationship behind it is naturally at risk because it is easier for customers to be critical of something they currently use and know as compared to something new and untried. That is the point of attack by the competition. You must continually validate and reinforce the key decision makers' support because the competition will continually snipe at the vulnerable people until they take the business away.

Three important customer types should be monitored during the relationship—people who have the organizational influence and political power to impact the relationship.

A

Alpha

Alpha is the first letter in the Greek alphabet; which symbolizes the beginning point in the relationship management. Therefore, the person assigned the lead role in the deal management is the Alpha manager. This is the point person, or champion, for the customer side of the contract and the ongoing relationship. In complex organizations this person is typically from the user group or a special contracts management team. If no apparent Alpha is assigned to the project, it is wise to negotiate with the customer organization to appoint a person to that role.

Ω

Omega

Omega is the last letter in the Greek alphabet, and symbolizes the *end* decision maker. The person assigned to make the ultimate budget or financial decisions in the deal is the Omega manager. Most business organizations have clear guidelines on budget control and signature authority for contracts. Thus the Omega Person has the ultimate *fiduciary responsibility* to the organization as it relates to your contract. Each organization has a different political structure that defines these limits; a vice president in one organization may not have as large a dollar limit as a manager in another organization.

Δ

Delta

Delta people in the customer organization can influence the other decision makers, particularly the Omega. They are referred to as *change agents* in the deal. Delta is the Greek letter used in scientific equations as the symbol for change, or difference.

These individuals or departments are often considered by some to have low impact on the relationship because they do not have the authority or title to sign the contract. However, this group most often unravels the deal. Their collective influence on the Omega can make or break the relationship.

As the organization becomes larger and more complex, the potential Deltas increase in number, are spread over more organizational levels and often these extend to different geographic locations. The chart in Figure 8.2 shows the possible organizational layers.

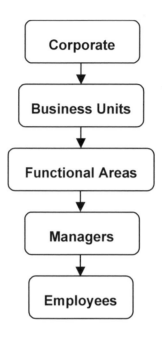

Figure 8.2

Deltas can come from a variety of functions and the most common departments involved are:

Finance

General Accounting

Accounts Payable

Accounts Receivable

Human Resources

Business Planning

Training

Research and Development

Operations
Production
Fulfillment
Customer Service
Purchasing
Information Systems
Technical Support/Service

Marketing/Sales
Product/Brand Manager
Installation/Customer Relations
Channel/Distributor Management

Executive Level
President/Executive Officers
Business Development
Corporate
Legal

Managing the sheer number of potential Deltas is daunting, but identifying the informal leaders of that group can simplify the task. In our process, these leaders among the Deltas are called *Bell Cows*. It is a concept I learned while growing up working on my uncle's dairy farm in western Pennsylvania. To keep track of his cows while they were grazing, my uncle tied a bell on the lead cow's collar because wherever that cow went, the herd followed. It was a simple but effective way to monitor the herd's location. The tricky part was to be sure you have the bell on the right cow. Here are the important rules my uncle taught me:

Bell Cow Rules

- The herd picks the lead cow, not the farmer.

- The lead cow takes everyone to the best hay or grazing.

- If you sell the lead cow, another cow will take her place and do exactly the same thing.

- The lead cow only loses credibility if she tells the herd you are coming with feed and it turns out you are not.

- Lead cows like to make you think the whole herd is hungry.

Group dynamics within organizations delineate people based on results achievement, and trust. The chart in Figure 8.3 illustrates this matrix.

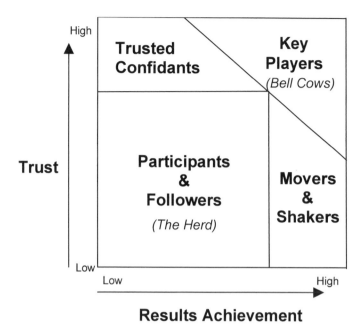

Figure 8.3

The group defines its leaders as the people known to have high trust levels within the group and who consistently produce results. The Key Players shape their group and often the entire organization culture through their influence and leadership. People naturally want to follow them because they are trusted winners. Increase your odds of maintaining the relationship by designing a tracking system to identify and monitor the correct Key Players (Bell Cows) among the Delta group.

Implementation Plan

Pre-signing (phase 1)

Have your team check the language of the contract. Minimal team review should encompass the legal, financial, and operational (production and delivery) aspects, as well as any other departments responsible for fulfilling the deal. Look for any items that could be questionable for either side.

Old school was that each side only looked out for their own interest. If the other side is not smart enough to catch this mistake, the lesson will be good for them! Why risk a short-term blunder that could cost the other side — even if it benefits you? It is better to negotiate the contract in good faith from the beginning because you are ultimately negotiating the *relationship*. Do not use *penny wise* tactics at this phase because they will make you *pound foolish*.

Sometimes in large complex deals, upfront documents are used to identify business deal terms before the definitive agreement is signed. Letter of Intent (LOI), Memorandum of Understanding (MOU), and Term Sheet are examples used by companies to identify whether or not they have common ground for a deal before they spend time and money to negotiate a full blown agreement. Additionally the Non Disclosure Agreement (NDA) is growing in use to protect trade secrets and intellectual property rights during this exploratory period.

Early stages - Mid contract and pre-renewal (Phase 2-3)

Review the contact and the implementation steps. Make sure the transition teams on both sides are comfortable with the process. Schedule the review dates, and at every opportunity review why the deal was done in the first place to keep the group focus on the big picture.

The business relationship is always tested during contract renewal. Either side may go back to a *competitive negotiation* style, and jockey for position to gain a little more profit in the next year. Most experienced negotiators relate that the other side develops *Temporary Alzheimer's* when it comes to the positive memories of the relationship. In fact, the tactic of *casting guilt* may be used as a leverage tool to focus on everything but the positives. A better way is to approach it like an employee review—each side should candidly discuss strengths and weaknesses, and develop action plans for improvement.

PUTTING IT ALL TOGETHER

Know Thy Self

Know Thy Customer

File Folder

Dialogue

Trust Revisited

"He who knows others is wise. He who knows himself is enlightened."

> \- Lao Tzu, Chinese Philosopher

Know Thy Self

"Know Thy Self" is one of the keys to understanding the true purpose of life. It is a tenet of almost every culture and religion throughout the world, encouraging us as individuals to understand who we are and what gifts we have in this life. To take this analogy to the business world, it simply means understanding what your organization is good at, and what "gift" your organization brings to the marketplace. Today, success in business revolves around this crucial insight into both your customer and your own organization. You need to know what your company embodies.

The three elements that help position an organization in its marketplace are:

1. A defining "Word" that summarizes the focus of your organization.

2. Triple Crown strengths and weaknesses.

3. A consistent "message" to customer, suppliers and employees.

Defining Word

Most successful organizations take the sum of their goals and values and distill it into one defining *"word."* Disney's word is *"happiness"* and it is clearly evident at Disney theme parks, each billed as "the happiest place on earth." Who Disney hires, what Disney develops, and how Disney conducts business, all spring from this core word; and it is one of the keys to their overwhelming success.

3M defines itself by the word *"innovation"*. Its corporate culture fosters employee creativity, giving employees the freedom to take risks and try new ideas. More than 50,000 innovative products developed by employees are the result of this core culture.

BASF's word is *"Verbund"*, which is the 'process' used across the entire organization (Figure 9.1). In 1865, Friedrich Engelhorn founded BASF, now one of the largest chemical conglomerates in the world. His vision was to bring dye research and production under one roof. Each production facility was linked to other plants so that the products and leftover material from one plant could serve as raw materials in the next. Today, over

350 plants form an integrated network connected by at least one product or process stage. At BASF, this efficient network is known as *"Verbund."* It is an integral part of their corporate philosophy. It sets the tone within the company and in dealings with customers, strategic partners, and the community as a whole.

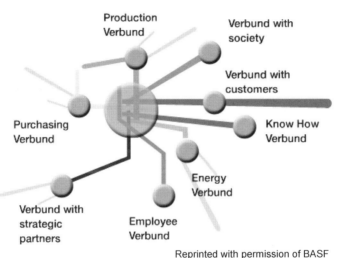

Reprinted with permission of BASF

Figure 9.1

What is your organization's defining *"word"*?

Triple Crown

Does each of the functional units in your organization understand how they impact the Triple Crown components? A flip-chart interactive exercise concerning each department's contributions to each of the Three Crowns is often a real eye-opener for employees. By utilizing the template shown in Figure 9.2, employees can visualize the unique contributions each of their departments make to their customers, and gain an understanding of their fit in the organization's grand scheme.

TRIPLE CROWN OF BUSINESS WORTH

Person People deal with people they trust and like	**Product** Logic and emotion of the deal	**Company** Stability and security of the relationship

Figure 9.2

Consistent Message

Companies that exalt their great customer service and open-door-honest communications with employees, and then conduct ruthless, unethical negotiations with suppliers, send a mixed and disturbing message. Ethics is not something that is applied only to specific situations. It is a consistent way of doing business. Becoming trustworthy depends on three attributes:

- Ability – are you good at what you do?

- Concern – do you care about me, or are you in it only for yourself?

- Integrity – do you have strong moral values?

You cannot fool people in either your company or the marketplace. An example of this is a company that wanted to conduct a survey of its employees to find ways to boost morale. They promised a confidential survey to get straight answers, but one of the employees discovered that the forms were marked on the back with a hidden code that identified the responding employee. Not only did the survey fail to gain valid responses, but now the employees mistrust management even more and morale is at an all time low.

A consistent culture based on trust is the foundation of successful organizations.

Know Thy Customer

The second part of the business success equation is, "Know Thy Customer." This does not mean having superficial information about your customer, but rather, gaining a deep understanding of your customer's business and how they make a profit. What are your customer's major products or services? Who are their customers? What is their distinct advantage in the market? Ask the questions that give you insight as to how you can help your customer's business succeed.

Understand the latest initiatives your customers are undertaking. Many organizations are adopting 6-Sigma, a quality quest based on disciplined use of fact-based, data-driven, decision-making. 6-Sigma is particularly important to suppliers because the customer will rely on the collective intelligence of all participants in their business to make significant process improvements. An example of this is Caterpillar. They adopted 6-Sigma in January 2001 and placed a section on their company Web site to alert everyone to this shift in business thinking. If you plan on doing business with Caterpillar you will need to understand this initiative or you will not make their "A" list of suppliers.

Focus on where your product or service can have the biggest impact on your customer's business strategy – at what functional level does your worth have impact? The universal functions of a business are listed below. Examine them for your own best fit in working with your customers for contributions to their:

1. Positive cash flow.

2. Customer niche.

3. Customer relationships.

Positive Cash Flow

All companies depend on making a profit. It is the life-blood of business survival. If you do not make a profit, and in a timely manner, you are not a business – you are a hobby. Someone should have reminded the dot-com-boom companies of this fundamental law because most of their business plans actually forecasted no profits – a fatal deviation from the first universal law of cash flow. The experts were not surprised by those failed ventures; what did surprise them was that people readily invested into such flawed schemes.

Negotiating the best deal to increase the bottom line, particularly through accelerating cash flow, is still a vital task of any business. Just-in-Time (JIT) inventory programs are able to free up precious capital for investments in other strategic areas. An example of this is the Dell Computer production facility: A yellow demarcation line separates the Dell side of the production floor from the side belonging to the supplier. As Dell builds a computer, inventory crosses the line only when needed, and Dell is invoiced for that product only, virtually eliminating inventory expenses.

Customers are also developing systems that benefit the supplier's cash flow. An example is Microsoft's Web-based invoicing system. As a supplier to Microsoft, we enter our invoices over a secure Web site and the payment is electronically transferred to our bank account, eliminating mailing delays and trips to the bank for manual deposits.

Defining Customer's Niche

The customer buys a composite or "package" (of goods & services), and it is not for the supplier to guess what the customer needs, but to understand what the customer actually *wants*. It is imperative to find out how your product or service can help your customer enhance their position in the market.

An example of this is the 2001 launch of the Ford Thunderbird. Considering all the negative press over the Ford Explorer and Firestone tire issues, coupled with the termination of Jacques Nasser CEO, the market was watching this launch with great concern. Joseph Philllippi, a Wall Street auto analyst summed it up with, *"This is clearly a hallmark vehicle, a "halo" vehicle. They absolutely cannot afford any quality issues or glitches on it. It's absolutely critical that they launch without a hitch."* Now imagine you are a supplier to Ford working on the M205 program (internal code name for Thunderbird). You are at a supplier quality-process-meeting where you are told that top Ford executives were embarrassed by problems with vehicle launches. It doesn't take a rocket scientist to figure out that Ford really *wants* a successful Thunderbird launch with no quality problems. Your task is to make that specific *want* a reality. The Thunderbird will enable Ford to regain prestige in the market, and contribute to its division's success. The supplier's contribution to help Ford define its market niche as a "Quality" automaker, overrides any other issues, including price.

Customer Relationships

Acquiring customers is expensive, but losing them is devastatingly more costly! A key part of the strategic plan of most organizations should be to engage with suppliers who can help keep customers. Even in economic downturns, the savvy consumers are spending, but looking for real value. Some growing practices include joint sponsorship of educational seminars with "end" customers. Coca-Cola sponsors programs to help organizations launch overseas expansions, tapping into their knowledge base of opening up foreign markets. Laguna Group partnered with Baxter, a major healthcare company, who sponsored training programs for hospitals on recruiting and hiring of talented medical workers. A similar program funded by Astra/Merck helped physicians by providing training programs on marketing and leadership roles on hospital boards. These are all examples of efforts to help enhance relationships with a customer's end-customer.

Many companies fail to realize that their vendors are potential customers, and often influence the overall market perception. HMO's and other managed-care organizations learned this the hard way. They brutalized their partners — hospitals and doctors — treating them like "commodity vendors" until the partners rebelled, often taking patients with them. The HMOs found that "gag clauses" in the doctors' contracts did not cover up the dichotomy they were presenting in the market. How could they care about patients and health, when the message was simply Price, Price, and Price? One HMO that had initials of FHP (Family Health Plan) was nicknamed as <u>F</u>urniture <u>H</u>as <u>P</u>riority -— by the employees!

The definition of *customer* has expanded to include suppliers and employees. The organizations that recognize this shift will prosper.

File Folder

Back in my senior year of high school, I bought the car of my dreams with money I saved from part-time jobs. It was a used 1965 Chevy Impala Super Sport – 396-cubic-inch engine, four-barrel carburetor, Hurst four-speed stick-shift, glass-packed mufflers, and yes, it was red! The main purpose of this story is to introduce you to a concept that I learned that year.

My dad congratulated me on my hard work in saving up for the car and said he wanted to give me something for the car. He gave me a file folder. Now don't get me wrong, it was a nice folder - manila in color and all. Not that I wasn't appreciative, but I was expecting something a little more substantial.

He said, "Frank, you just bought a nice car and I know you will take great care of it. I want you to take this file folder and any time you do anything to this car, put a receipt in here. When you change the oil, tune it up, or do any maintenance to it, make a note or put the receipt in this folder. When you go to sell this car, just telling people that you maintained it well won't impress them. Show them the proof, pull out this folder and show them the receipts, and your maintenance records. That will get you top dollar when you sell it."

My dad was right. Every car that I have owned, I got high blue-book when I sold it, mainly from keeping good records in the file folder. That advice made me a profit on my car sales, but it really paid off a lot more when I transferred that concept to my business career.

Keeping records is permanent proof of quality work. A file folder will help keep track of the high points of the relationship. It is important that you constantly find out what is important to the other side, and document your progress toward those goals. Remember that people forget, things change, and the initial passion and excitement may not be there later in the relationship. People tend to focus on the *"issue de jour."* It is a common, but very human fault to think more about the "now" problems than positive past history. The form in Figure 9.3 is one way to develop a plan, take action and have a record of accomplishments.

Contract/Relationship Validation and Action Planning

Commitment	Timing	Ownership Customer Supplier	Milestone	Deliverable / Measurement

Figure 9.3

How to Track the Triple Crown

The investment an organization makes in building value in all three components, the Person, the Product, and the Company, pays off in lasting relationships and loyalty. The danger with focusing on only one Crown is that it lacks balance. The customer needs to have *Worth* in all three areas.

In 1986, Gerber had reports of slivers of glass in their jars of baby food. A public-relations nightmare ensued, even though there were no serious injuries. Gerber recovered sales and confidence by 1988, but they have made it very clear to the glass-bottle manufacturers that they deal with — they do not want to repeat it ever again. Gerber promised the glass industry: One more incident of glass slivers in baby food, and we will switch to plastic overnight! One of the companies competing for Gerber's business was Owens-Brockway. They had excellent manufacturing processes and top-notch people, but they were always concerned that their customers may not have the passion to understand their commitment to quality. Owens-Brockway adopted my

Triple Crown program and trained all functional areas on the concepts — they even went so far as to track all customer contacts to see if they were building value in all three areas consistently. Here is an example of a customer-contact tracking system that they used:

Customer Contact Tracking:

Date	Decision Maker	Person Responsible	Milestone or Objective	Triple Crown ☺ ® 🏢			Outcome
3/2	Gates/Finance	Williams	Initiate secure Web Site order processing			√	Successful implementation
4/1	Curran/Production	Lee	Discuss & smooth out late shipment	√		√	Lunch and plant tour, OK now
4/2	Curran/Production	McCoy	Demonstrate new tooling		√		Positive feedback

Triple Crown Symbol Key:
☺ = Person   ® = Product   🏢 = Company

Figure 9.4

This mechanism to track Triple Crown events can be incorporated into most currently available contact-management software (i.e., ACT, Outlook, Goldmine) to aid in entry and report generation. Viewing Triple Crown activities over time provides a telltale early-warning system of potentially weak areas. We have noticed that people gravitate toward a favorite Crown and often neglect the other two in their routine activities. Some "techies" love to talk technical product specifications and performance (Product Crown), often forgetting to reinforce the Company Crown. Some salespeople rely too heavily on bonding and social activities (People Crown), neglecting to reinforce Product and Company Crowns. A visual scan of the customer report will demonstrate the focus of activities over time and will reveal balance, or lack of, in the three Crowns.

This mechanism enables continuity and reinforcement of the original value-proposition that gained the business relationship and can sustain it in phases two and three.

Dialogue

The *Give-Get Alliance Model* is a way of discussing the business relationship with the purpose of continually fostering commitment from both parties. This tool is a visual template to share with key decision-makers, defining each side's contributions and benefits, enabling a two-way dialogue on the relationship.

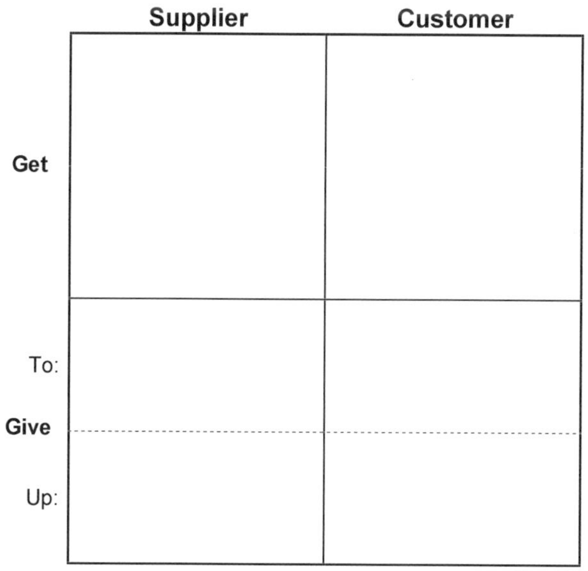

	Supplier	**Customer**
Get		
To:		
Give		
Up:		

Figure 9.5

Important points to remember:
- The key people make business deals work.
- It will take time and resources to make it last – from both sides.
- Each side must reach the threshold of significant trust, or it won't work.
- Use the Give – Get Alliance Model to balance the relationship and prevent resentment.

The Give-Get Alliance Model shifts relationships and the contract to a higher level of commitment. The term, compliance, hints of adhering to the "letter of the law" in the contract, or doing the minimum required. Commitment implies a stronger attitude, one that promises to live up to the spirit of the agreement. A graphic example of the old one-sided Give-Take style vs. the two-way dialogue Give-Get style of negotiation and the resulting effect on commitment is demonstrated in Figure 9.6.

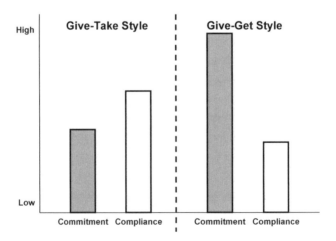

Figure 9.6

Trust Revisited

The Three Stages of Business Trust

Earn

Organizations must initiate specific actions and strategies to minimize suspicious, antagonistic, or deceptive negotiating tactics. They must develop consistent and honest "honeymoon" communications with customers, suppliers and employees. Far too often, we see a company talk about honest and ethical behavior, yet they do not "walk the talk" when dealing with suppliers or stakeholders. This leaves employees confused as to what the real message is. Often the employees' response is to lose trust in their own organization, which can lead to serious or even catastrophic consequences.

The legal profession is wonderfully prepared during law school for adversarial litigation. Only recently are these schools starting to reshape their curriculum to business-relationship law. It is a profound shift from the thinking of "what's the maximum we can do to legally protect our clients' interests and our interests only," to "let's protect our interests, but be fair in the process." The first often gave the impression of *deal prevention* with its Draconian ways and somewhat deceptive clauses. The second way implies that *deal retention* is a high priority, lightening of the "heavy hand" in the contract language to a realistic workable document.

Transfer

The original architects of the deal often move on to work on other projects, accept promotions, or even leave the company. Keeping trust and the relationship active requires the development of a cohesive plan to transfer the stewardship of the relationship over time. The people managing the relationship need to keep the agreement principles constantly visible so each side remembers why the original deal was struck. It is important to constantly reinforce the original "value-proposition" and the Triple Crown relationship sustaining elements.

Lost

Every business deal will end sometime. Planning to prevent the unexpected catastrophic event from ending it prematurely is a wise investment. There is a direct link between high trust levels and organizations surviving random product and performance shortcomings. Trust in business is fragile and history shows it can be lost in the blink of an eye.

Congratulations on making it this far in my book, for that you deserve one more entertaining story. This is a humorous example of how trust of lawyers is viewed. It is also a cautionary tale that gets to the point of maintaining trust, whatever profession you are in. The story involves a defense attorney who was cross-examining a police officer during a felony trial — it went like this:

> ATTORNEY: Officer, did you see my client fleeing the scene?
>
> ANSWER: No, sir. But I subsequently observed a person matching the description of the offender running several blocks away.
>
> ATTORNEY: Officer, who provided this description?

ANSWER: The officer who responded to the scene.

ATTORNEY: A fellow officer provided the description of this so-called offender. Do you trust your fellow officers?

ANSWER: Yes, sir — with my life.

ATTORNEY: With your life? Let me ask you this then, officer. Do you have a locker room in the police station — a room where you change your clothes in preparation for your daily duties?

ANSWER: Yes, sir. We do.

ATTORNEY: And do you have a locker in that room?

ANSWER: Yes, sir. I do.

ATTORNEY: And do you have a lock on your locker?

ANSWER: Yes, sir. I do.

ATTORNEY: Now why is it, officer, if you trust your fellow officers with your life that you find it necessary to lock your locker in a room you share with those same officers?

ANSWER: You see, sir, we share the building with a court complex, and sometimes lawyers have been known to walk through that room.

With that, the courtroom erupted in laughter and a prompt recess was called.

Unfortunately, negotiating strategy and tactics have lagged in development for some organizations. Contracts and deals are often conducted on the simple level like that of Colo the gorilla, trading bits of the charm bracelet for a piece of fruit — then repeating the same procedure over and over again. May you be so lucky to have those organizations as your competitors, and may you prosper by evolving with the changing times as a result of the concepts in this book.

ABOUT THE AUTHOR

Frank Kondrot is a leading business consultant and the founder of Laguna Group, a globally recognized firm specializing in performance improvement for corporations and key executives.

Frank delivers high value to his clients based on the breadth of his business experience. Throughout his career of more than 20 years at senior-level corporate management positions with prominent corporations as 3M, Baxter Healthcare, and Carter Wallace, he has managed large national staffs and sales organizations, successfully guiding new market growth and exceeding profit goals. Frank is renowned as one of the nation's top business negotiation experts. Fortune 500 companies regularly call him to assist in assessing and reshaping the way they do business to enhance customer relationships and profits.

Over the years Frank Kondrot has built a reputation as a leading business speaker and motivator on topics including negotiating, leadership, coaching, and strategic alliances. Frank offers a unique blend of business experience with an ability to inspire, engage and motivate his audience.

His style is practical, and he is passionate about his audience achieving results. His popularity, public speaking ability and humor make him one of the most sought after business speakers in the country.

Frank holds a B.S. Degree in Biology and Chemistry from the University of Pittsburgh in Pennsylvania. He has completed post-graduate courses in Business Administration and holds a Certificate in Management from the University of California, Irvine. He is a member of the Association for Professional Consultants, Professional Coaches and Mentors and the National Speakers Association.

For more information on consulting, seminars or keynote speeches offered by Frank Kondrot through Laguna Group, please contact him at:

fkondrot@lagunagroup.com

Laguna Group
Laguna Niguel, California
Telephone: (949) 240-9069
Fax: (949) 240-9032

www.lagunagroup.com

Index

Laguna Group Winning Edge® Seminars

The Laguna Group has extensively researched the characteristics of the best of the best in business – the companies and their leaders, resulting in our Winning Edge programs. They contain the practical and effective skills that enable your organization to thrive in today's changing business climate.

Laguna Group is passionate about client results. The firm helps clients impact the bottom line and improve business effectiveness. Laguna Group is in business to see its clients win.

The firm's signature is stimulating, interactive, practical seminars. Programs are custom-designed for each client, not off-the-shelf, generic sessions.

Every business is different, and Laguna Group creates solutions to match each customer. The firm researches a client's industry, market conditions, opportunities and customers to design programs that reflect the actual business environment. We get to the heart of a client's business and present the strategies and tactics for success.

For more information.

Phone: **(800) 8 Laguna**

Email: **seminars@lagunagroup.com**

Or visit our web site: **www.lagunagroup.com**

To Order Additional Copies

Phone orders: (949) 240-9069. Have your credit card ready.

Fax orders: (949) 240-9032. Use form below.

Mail orders: Laguna Group, Inc. 30251 Golden Lantern #108, Laguna Niguel, CA 92677

Internet orders: Purchase directly from our website at
www.lagunagroup.com

FAX / MAIL FORM (Use copier to duplicate)

Name: _____

Title: _____

Company: _____

Address: _____

City: _____State: ____Zip: _____

Telephone: (_____) _____ - _____

Fax: (___) _____-_____

Email: _____

Number of books requested_____

Payment: VISA__ MasterCard __

Card#_____

Name on card: _____ Exp. Date: ____/____

Signature_____

Sales tax: 7.75% will be added to books shipped within California.
Shipping: $4 will be added for the first book, $2 for each additional book.